THE LITTLE FLOWERS OF ST. FRANCIS

The Little Flowers of Saint Francis

The Acts of Saint Francis and His Companions

Translated by
Professor E. M. Blaiklock
and Professor A. C. Keys

SERVANT BOOKS
Ann Arbor, Michigan

Cover Illustration by Giotto. Courtesy Scalla/Art
Resource, NY

Published by Servant Books
P.O. Box 8617
Ann Arbor, Michigan 48107

Original edition published in 1985 by Hodder &
Stoughton, London

Library of Congress Cataloging in Publication Data

Actus Beati Francisci et sociorum ejus. English.
  The little flowers of St. Francis.

  Translation of: Acuts Beati Francisci et sociorum ejus.
  Editor: Paul Sabatier.
  1. Francis, of Assisi, Saint, 1182-1226—Legends.
I. Blaiklock, E.M. II. Keys, A.C. III. Sabatier,
Paul, 1858-1928. IV. Title. V. Title: Little flowers
of Saint Francis.
BX4700.F62E5 1986   271'.3'024   85-30396
ISBN 0-89283-300-9

Contents

Preface

THIS TRANSLATION of the *Acts of Saint Francis and his Companions* comprises all seventy-six chapters of the Latin text edited and first published in 1902 by Paul Sabatier, a biographer of Saint Francis. Some fifty-three chapters, in modified form and translated into Italian, together with additional material, were incorporated into the better-known *Little Flowers of Saint Francis,* which belong to the later fourteenth century. The old theory that these *Fioretti* were a translation of a hypothetical *Floretum* (Latin for anthology) is now discredited. To the original *Fioretti* of the fifty-three chapters was later added material from at least five different sources. All this enhances the value and interest of the original *Actus Sancti Francisci et sociorum eius.* The author of most (not all) of the *Actus* was Brother Ugolino da Monte Santa Maria, writing some hundred years after the death of Saint Francis (1182-1226).

Saint Francis was born in the little town of Assisi, the son of a prosperous merchant. History would have it that he was travelling on business in France when his son was born and the mother named her new born son John, in honor of the well-loved disciple, but upon returning with rich profits, he re-named him Francis after the country which had been the scene of his recent success! Thus from the start legends and stories abound about this remarkable man whose ministry still has a great impact.

However, the first twenty-four years of his life were spent in luxury as he indulged his taste for fun and splendor, winning the sobriquet of the "flower of youth." When he reached twenty-four, a war between the city states of Assisi and Perugia broke out. Francis was taken prisoner and languished in captivity for over a year. Once freed, he returned home, but suffered from various illnesses for a period of years. He had ample time to think and began to long for a sense of purpose and meaning to his life.

It was the great age of chivalry, and at first he dreamt of riding out to redress wrong and crusade for the poor and weak. Gradually, he began to devote himself to the poor and the sick, being particularly touched by the abject poverty of the lepers, of whom there were many at that time.

He embarked diligently on his new-found mission and within a period of two years restored three churches and gained twelve disciples, the first being Bernard of Quintavalle. Within eleven years the Brothers grew to more than five thousand, all having taken a vow of abject poverty. This total negation of the material world and its possessions differentiated the Franciscans from all other ecclesiastical bodies of the time.

Francis also founded the Order of Poor Ladies, known as the Poor Clares, in honor of their first abbess. Later still the Third Order was established, open to both sexes, and meant for those wishing to live in the world, rather than in Monastic communities. All three orders spread rapidly and their influence endures today.

The chief quality of Saint Francis is the depth and tenderness of his kind heart. His spiritual fervor, fasting, visions and utterances may seem somewhat removed to modern man. The lessons and truths they convey are, however, eternal. The objects of his exuberant love were not only God, angels, and men, but also animals, birds, insects and even inanimate objects, which he often addressed as brothers and sisters.

Surely his compassion for the poor, the sick and the lowly, his total disinterest in material possessions, and his striving to worship and please God, are even more relevant to us today than they were in medieval Italy.

Editor's Note

PROFESSOR BLAIKLOCK DIED ON OCTOBER 26, 1983, having completed roughly half the translation. He had felt tired through the summer of that year, and finally cancer was to get the better of him. He died surrounded by his family, courteous and appreciative to the end. He insisted on carrying on with the translation until mid-October when he became too fatigued. It has been a great privilege to work with him on this, his final book, the eighty-first in a busy career.

Finally, we would also like to express our appreciation to Professor A. C. Keys, who so graciously and willingly undertook the task of revising and completing the translation. Without his hard work, this book would never have been published.

Chapter 1

To the praise and glory of our Lord Jesus Christ and the holy Father Francis. The record of certain notable facts concerning Francis and his companions and certain remarkable deeds of theirs which have been passed by in the legends concerning him and which are also profitable and devout.

FIRST, IT MUST BE BORNE IN MIND that our blessed master Saint Francis in everything he did was like Christ. Just as Christ, at the beginning of his ministry, chose twelve apostles who abandoned all things, so the blessed Francis had twelve picked companions who chose the most abject poverty. And just as one of the apostles hanged himself, so one of the companions mentioned, Brother John of Capella, hanged himself. And just as they were a source of wonder to the whole world and full of the Holy Spirit, so those most holy companions of the holy Francis were men of such saintliness that the world has never seen their like since the time of the apostles. One of their number was caught up to the third heaven, to wit, Brother Giles, and one, Brother Philip Longus, was touched on the lips like Isaiah with a burning coal. One, Brother Silvester, used to speak to God as friend with friend, so unsullied was his person. One would wing his way like an eagle to the light of God's wisdom, to wit, Brother Bernard, that most humble man, who explained the Scriptures most profoundly. Another was sanctified by God and canonized in heaven while still living in this world. This was Brother Ruffino, as though made

1

holy before birth, a man most faithful to Christ, a nobleman of Assisi. So all shone with a special privilege, as will appear in what follows. Of them all the firstborn and foremost in point of time and outstanding sanctity was Brother Bernard of Assisi who was converted thus . . .

While Saint Francis was still in layman's clothing, although he had already renounced the worldly hopes of men, he would go about so unkempt and careless of his person, that by many he was considered mad, seasoned though he was by God's salt and grounded in the peace of the Holy Spirit. As he went about Assisi, he was persecuted physically and pelted with both mud and stones by his own townsmen and hosts of strangers. Yet with the utmost patience and a happy face he went through it all as if he were deaf and dumb. But Master Bernard of Assisi, one of the noblest, richest and wisest men in the city, whose advice all respected, began wisely to think about such profound contempt for the world as he saw in Saint Francis, such constancy under persecution, and such long suffering in endurance. Though for two years he had been so hated and despised by men, he seemed ever more steadfast. Then said Master Bernard in his heart: "It cannot but be that this Francis has great grace from God."

Inspired by God, he invited Saint Francis to sup with him one night. Saint Francis humbly accepted the invitation. Master Bernard had it in mind to look closely into the holiness of Saint Francis, and so invited him to sleep that night in his home. When Saint Francis humbly accepted, he had a bed made up for him in his own room, in which a lamp was always burning at night. Saint Francis, as soon as he entered the room, in order to conceal the divine grace that he had, immediately threw himself on the bed, as though he wished to sleep, but Master Bernard had in mind to watch him secretly at night. That is why he used this subterfuge. Shortly after settling in bed, he pretended to fall into a deep sleep and to snore prodigiously.

But Saint Francis, faithful guardian of the secrets of God, when he judged that Master Bernard was fast asleep, in the deep stillness of night rose from his bed. With face turned to heaven, and hands and eyes lifted to God, in complete surrender and with the warmest devotion he prayed, saying: "My God, my All." These words he groaned out to God with copious tears, again and again with solemn devotion until dawn: "My God, my All"—no more. So said Saint Francis, worshipping God's Majesty, which seemed to stoop to the imperilled world and provide a remedy for the salvation of the poor through his own Son. Enlightened by the spirit of prophecy, and foreseeing the mighty deeds God was about to do through his own Order, and considering in the same spirit's teaching his own insufficiency and poverty of virtue, he was calling on God to do himself what he was unable to do. Without such aid, man's frailty is powerless. Hence his words: "My God, my All."

But Master Bernard, the lamp being still alight, saw everything. Carefully, and with urgent attention, he weighed the words quoted. In his heart of hearts he was deeply moved by the Holy Spirit, and as soon as morning came, he called Saint Francis and said to him: "Brother Francis, I am fully determined to abandon this world, and to follow you wherever you command." Saint Francis heard and rejoiced in spirit. He said: "Master Bernard, this is a task so difficult that the guidance of our Lord Jesus Christ must be sought, so that he himself may be pleased to make known his good will to us, and how we must bring this to pass. Let us therefore go to the bishop's house where there is a good priest. We shall ask for mass to be said and, when we have heard it we shall pray until the third hour. In our prayer we shall seek of our Lord Jesus Christ graciously to show us, in three openings of the missal, what it is his good pleasure for us to do." Master Bernard said: "Be it as you say."

3

So they went to the bishop's house, and when mass had been heard, and prayer continued to the third hour, the priest took up the missal as Saint Francis and Master Bernard requested. Protecting himself with the sign of the Cross, he opened the Gospel in the name of our Lord Jesus Christ. At the first opening he encountered: "If you wish to be perfect, go and sell all that you have and give it to the poor." At the second opening he encountered: "Let him who would come after me deny himself and take up his cross . . ." The third time he encountered: "Take nothing for your journey." When these words had been read, Saint Francis said to Master Bernard: "See the guidance we have of the Lord. Go and do exactly as you have heard. And blessed be our Lord Jesus Christ who has deigned to show us the way of the Gospel."

Immediately Master Bernard sold off all his possessions, which were of very great value, and distributed all to the poor, carrying a wallet full of money, which he distributed among widows, orphans, pilgrims and the servants of God, richly and generously, with Saint Francis joining in and faithfully helping the whole proceeding.

But Master Silvester, when he saw this dispersal of property, prompted by greed said to Saint Francis: "You have not fully paid my account for some stone for church repairs." Saint Francis, amazed at his greed, and not wishing to argue with him, as a true observer of the Gospel who gives to all who ask, put his hand into Bernard's purse and put a handful of money into Silvester's purse with the words: "If you ask for more, I will give it." Contented, he departed and returned home; but in the evening when he recalled what he had done that day, he reproached himself for his greed, and pondered on the fervor of Master Bernard and the holiness of Saint Francis. That night, and again the night afterward, and the night after that, he had a vision of a golden cross, proceeding from the mouth of Francis. Its top touched the sky and its arms seemed to reach the limits of the world. Thus touched by God, he realized all his assets and gave everything to the poor. Later, becoming a friar minor, he showed such holiness and grace, that he spoke with God as friend with friend, an experience which Saint Francis had, as will be demonstrated.

Master Bernard, with all his goods disposed of for God, and now leading a life of evangelical poverty, earned such grace from God that he was often caught up to the Lord. Saint Francis pronounced him worthy of all reverence, and would declare that it was he who had founded the order, in that it was he who first showed true evangelical poverty by distributing all he had to the poor, keeping absolutely nothing for himself, offering himself stripped of all to the arms of the Crucified, who is blessed for ever and ever. Amen.

Chapter 2

The humility and obedience of Saint Francis and Brother Bernard.

THAT MOST DEVOTED SERVANT OF CHRIST, Francis, because of the severity of his penance and continual weeping became almost blind so that he could scarcely see. So once, he left his dwelling place and went to visit Brother Bernard. Bernard was in a wood totally lost in divine contemplation and united with God. Saint Francis reached the wood and called Brother Bernard, saying: "Come and talk with this blind man." But Brother Bernard, since he was a man of deep contemplation, and at the moment was joined in spirit with God, did not reply to Saint Francis, nor go to him. Brother Bernard, in speaking with God, had extraordinary grace, as Francis had often experienced. That, in fact, is why he wanted to talk to him. So, after a short space of time, he called a second and a third time, repeating the same words: "Come and talk with this blind man." Neither time did Brother Bernard hear him, so that he neither came nor spoke to Saint Francis. So Saint Francis withdrew, somewhat put out and grieved in spirit that Brother Bernard, though called three times by him, had been unwilling to come.

Saint Francis, thinking such thoughts as he went away, said to his companions: "Wait for me a little while." And while he was giving himself to prayer in a quiet place alone, God made answer to him thus: "Why should you be put out, poor miserable little man? Should a man leave God for any human being? Brother Bernard, when you were calling him, was in full communion with me, and so was not able to come to you or make reply. So do not wonder that he was not able to come to you or reply to you. He was in such ecstasy that he simply did not hear what you said."

Understanding this, Saint Francis immediately went in haste back to Brother Bernard, humbly to blame himself for his earlier thoughts. But Brother Bernard, that true saint, hurried to meet Saint Francis and fell at his feet. And the humility of Saint Francis, and the love and reverence of Brother Bernard, met each with each. Telling of the rebuke he had received from God, Saint Francis bade Brother Bernard do in obedience whatever he directed. Fearing Saint Francis might impose on him too heavy a demand, as he often did, wishing to leave a way to refuse, he said sincerely: "I am prepared, father, to obey you provided you obey me also in what I shall direct." "I agree," said Saint Francis. And Brother Bernard: "You may say, father, what you wish me to do." Saint Francis said: "In the name of holy obedience, I bid you punish the presumptuousness and the boldness of my heart; as I lie on the ground, place one foot on my throat and one on my mouth and tread back and forth three times, saying: 'Lie there, boorish son of Pietro Bernardone.' And other great maledictions shall you heap on me saying: 'Whence this arrogance of yours, vilest creature?'" Bernard found it hard to do what he had heard. However, for obedience' sake, he did as he was bidden with the utmost care. This done, Saint Francis said: "Now, Brother Bernard, your orders, since I promised you obedience." Brother Bernard replied: "I bid you in the name of your obedience, whenever we are together, that you correct and rebuke me more sharply for all my faults." Saint Francis was amazed at this, because Brother Bernard was of such holiness that Saint Francis held him in the utmost reverence. That is why from then on Saint Francis was careful not to spend too long with him lest, because of his obedience, he should be required perhaps to utter rebuke against one he knew to be so godly a soul. And when he wanted to see Brother Bernard or to speak to him of God, he would leave him abruptly and hastily. It was a wonder to see how they vied each with the other, the one with the father, the other with his firstborn son, as love and obedience, patience and humility of each other faced the other. Praise and glory to God.

Chapter 3

How an angel accompanied Brother Bernard across a river.

IN THE EARLY DAYS of the Order, when there were few brothers and no friaries, Saint Francis went on a pilgrimage to the shrine of Saint James taking with him a few companions, one of whom was Brother Bernard. When they were travelling together they found in a certain country a man who was ill. Pitying him, Saint Francis said to Brother Bernard: "I want you, son, to stay and look after this sick man." Immediately, on bended knees and bowed head, he gave reverent obedience to the holy father. Saint Francis, leaving Brother Bernard with the sick man, went to Saint James's shrine with the other companions. While they stood in worship there, it was revealed to Saint Francis that he should found friaries throughout the world, so that his Order should expand into a great host. That is why, from then on, by God's command, he began to establish friaries everywhere.

On the way back by the same road, he found Brother Bernard and the sick man entrusted to his care in perfect health. So the following year Saint Francis allowed Brother Bernard to make a pilgrimage alone to Saint James's shrine. Meanwhile, Saint Francis returned to the valley of Spoleto, where he, Brother Masseo and Brother Elias, and certain others, dwelt in a remote place. Once Saint Francis went into a wood to pray. His companions, who held him in great reverence, all feared to interrupt his prayers because of the great revelations God made to him at such times.

It came about that a very handsome young man, dressed as if for travelling, came to the door, and knocked impatiently and long—an unusual occurrence. Going to the door, Brother Masseo said to the young man: "Son, I do not think you have ever been to a friary door before, because you do not know how to knock gently." The young man asked: "How should it be done?" Brother Masseo said: "Knock three times at short intervals, one knock after the other. Then wait until someone can say a paternoster and come to you. If he does not come in that time, knock again." The young man answered: "But I am in a great hurry. That is why I knock as I do, for I have a long way to go. I have come here to speak with Brother Francis, but he at the moment is meditating in the wood, and I do not wish to disturb him. But go and send Brother Elias to me. I have heard he is very wise, and I have a question for him."

Brother Masseo told Brother Elias to go to him, but he was annoyed, and in proud anger would not go. Brother Masseo did not know what to do, for he would be lying if he said Brother Elias could not come, but if he said he was angry and would not come, he was afraid he might set a bad example. And because meanwhile he delayed his returning, the young man knocked in the same fashion as before. Then Brother Masseo came to the door and said to the young man: "You did not knock as I told you to." But the young man was an angel of God and, anticipating Brother Masseo's answer, said: "Brother Elias does not wish to come to me, but do you go to Brother Francis and you will say that I have come to speak to him, but because I do not wish to disturb him, you are to tell him to send Brother Elias." So Brother Masseo went to Saint Francis as he was praying in the wood with his face lifted heavenward, and reported exactly what the young man had bidden, and Brother Elias's reply. Saint Francis, without moving from where he stood or lowering his face from heaven, said: "Go and tell Brother Elias to go to him under the terms of his obedience." Brother Elias came to the door in a bad temper, opened it violently with a great noise, and asked: "What do you want?" But the young man said: "Beware, dear, dear friend, for you seem to be in a bad temper, and anger hampers the soul and prevents it from seeing the truth." Then Brother Elias said: "Say what you want." "I ask you," he said, "whether the followers of the holy Gospel are permitted, as Christ said, to eat what is set before them, and whether anyone is allowed to impose on them things contrary to evangelical liberty?" Brother Elias replied haughtily: "I know those things well enough. I will not answer you. Go about your business." The young man said: "I could answer that question better than you." Brother Elias slammed the door and went away. Later he began to think about the question and to have doubts about it, for since he was vicar of the Order, he had presumed, exceeding the Gospel and the Rule, to command, and to draw up a direction that no brother in the Order should eat any kind of meat; so that the question was definitely aimed at him. So when he was unable to clarify his thoughts, he thought over that young man's modesty; and because he had said that he was better able to unravel the question than he was himself, he returned to the door and opened it, that he might ask to have the young man's solution from himself. But when he opened the door there was no one to be seen, nor could he be found after a general search. In fact, the young man was an angel of God, who departed because of him and because he was not welcomed. For a haughty mind is not worthy of conversing with an angel.

At this, Saint Francis, to whom everything had been revealed, returned from the wood, and sharply and loudly rebuked Brother Elias: "Brother Elias," he said, "you do wrong and arrogantly, too, who turn away holy angels, who come to visit and teach us. I tell you that I very much fear that this haughtiness of yours will put you out of the Order." And so later on it fell out, as Saint Francis in the spirit of prophecy foretold.

But on the same day and hour as the angel left Brother Elias, he appeared in the same guise to Brother Bernard as he was returning from Saint James's shrine, and stood on the bank of a great river which he could not cross. Greeting Brother Bernard in his own language, he said: "God grant you peace, good brother." Brother Bernard, noticing how handsome he was, the familiar language, peaceful salutation and joyous countenance, asked him: "Where do you come from, good young man?" "I come from the place where Saint Francis lives," he replied. "I came to talk with him but was not able, for he was in a wood pondering on the things of God. And staying with him there were the brethren Masseo,

Giles and Elias. Brother Masseo taught me how to knock at your door; Brother Elias, because he was too contemptuous to listen to the question I had for him, was not able to do so later when he thought better of it." Saying this, the angel said to Brother Bernard: "Why, dearest man, do you hesitate to cross the river?" He replied: "Because I fear danger from the depth of the waters before my eyes." The angel said: "Let us go over together. Do not hesitate." And taking his hand, in the twinkling of an eye, he placed Brother Bernard on the other side. Thus discerning that he was an angel of the Lord, Bernard said with great devotion, reverence and joy: "Blessed angel of God, tell me what is your name." He replied: "Why do you enquire my name, which is marvellous?" So saying, he vanished, and left Brother Bernard deeply comforted so that he walked the rest of his journey with joy.

Bernard himself noted the day and the hour of the angel's appearance to him, and when he came to the place where Saint Francis and his companions already mentioned were staying, he told the whole story in detail. So they quite confidently concluded that it was the same angel who had appeared to them and to him on the same day.

Chapter 4

How Brother Bernard went to Bologna.

SINCE OUR BLESSED FATHER FRANCIS, along with his companions, had been called by God to bear the Cross as much as to preach it, he and the pioneers of his Order seemed, as indeed they were, men truly crucified. Bearing the Crucified in dress, food and in

11

all their doings, desiring rather the reproach of Christ than the empty things of the world and its treacherous blandishments, they rejoiced in sufferings and held honor in contempt. They went through the world like pilgrims and strangers carrying nothing with them but Christ, for whose sake, wherever they went, because they were the living branches of the true vine, they bore choice fruit for Christ—the souls of men.

Thus it happened that, in the early days of the Order, Saint Francis sent Brother Bernard to Bologna, that there he might produce fruit for God, according to the grace given him. Brother Bernard, strengthening himself with the Cross of Christ, and with virtue linked to obedience, came to Bologna.

Some children saw him in his unusual and miserable dress, and began to heap insults on him. Brother Bernard, true saint that he was, not only bore them patiently, but even suffered them with deepest joy, because he was a true disciple of Christ who became "the scorn of the crowd and shame of men." For the love of Christ he deliberately placed himself in the marketplace of the city, where he could be the greatest object of the people's ridicule. One tugged at his hood from behind, another from the front, one threw dust, another stones. They pushed him this way and that. Bernard endured all this violence joyfully and patiently, without resistance in word or deed. What is more, in order to endure such persecution day after day, he would deliberately return to the same place. Whatever violence was heaped on him by them, he remained calm in spirit and with joyous face. Because patience is a work and demonstration of perfection, a wise judge, watching and thinking of such virtuous constancy undisturbed for so many days, said to himself: "It is quite obvious that this is a holy man." So, coming up to Brother Bernard, he asked: "Who are you and why did you come here?" Brother Bernard put his hand in the fold of his robe and produced the Gospel Rule of Saint Francis, which he carried in his

12

heart, and demonstrated by what he did. The judge, when he had read through the sublime statement of the Rule, was utterly amazed, for he was an intelligent man. Turning to his friends, he said in deep amazement: "This is the loftiest statement I have ever seen. This man and his colleagues are the holiest men on earth. They commit great sin who misuse them, and this man is to be treated not with violence, but the highest honors for he is indeed a friend of the All Highest." To Bernard he said: "Dearest man, if I showed you a suitable place where you could serve God fitly and are willing to receive it, I would most gladly give it to you for the salvation of my soul." Brother Bernard answered: "Dearest Master, I believe that the Lord inspired you to do this." Then the judge took Brother Bernard home with joy and great love, and showed him the house he had promised, and set it up at his own expense perfectly and devoutly.

He became the champion and the chief patron of Brother Bernard and his associates. Brother Bernard, on account of his holy way of life, began to be honored of men to the point that they counted themselves happy to touch, hear or see him.

Brother Bernard, indeed, truly humble disciple of Christ that he was, fearing that the honor shown him would hinder his peace and salvation, departed, returned to Saint Francis and said: A place is secured in Bologna where you sent me, father, so send brethren to live there, because I can do no further good there. Indeed, because of the great honor which is shown me, I fear to lose more than I gain." So the blessed Francis, hearing the full story of what the Lord had done through Brother Bernard, rejoicing and exulting in spirit, began to praise the Most High who had thus begun to spread abroad the poor little disciples of the Cross for the salvation of the people. So he chose members of the Order to send to Lombardy, and, as the devotion of the faithful grew, they established friaries everywhere. To God's praise.

Chapter 5

The gentle death of Brother Bernard.

OF SUCH HOLINESS was Brother Bernard that Saint Francis in his lifetime held him in deepest reverence, and often spoke in highest praise of him. It happened one day, when Saint Francis was in deep and earnest prayer, that God revealed to him that he was about to allow Brother Bernard to suffer many sharp assaults of the Devil. And Saint Francis thought with compassion of a Brother so beloved, and for many days with tears commended Brother Bernard to the Lord Jesus Christ asking that he would deign to give him victory over so many treacherous attacks. While Saint Francis was praying anxiously and earnestly thus, God's answer was made clear to him: "Brother, do not be afraid, because all the temptations to which Brother Bernard will be exposed are sent as a test of virtue and for the winning of a crown, and in the end he will joyfully carry the palm of victory over all those who assail him. Brother Bernard is one of those who shall be of the household of God." Saint Francis rejoiced at this reply, giving heartfelt thanks to Jesus Christ. From that moment he had neither doubt nor fear any more, and held Brother Bernard in ever deeper affection and regard, not only in life but at his death, as he showed.

So, when Saint Francis was on the point of death, like the patriarch Jacob, his sons standing around devoutly weeping at the departure of a father so beloved, Saint Francis said: "Where is my firstborn? Come, my son, that my soul may bless you before I die." Then Brother Bernard said quietly to Brother Elias, who was then vicar of the Order: "Father, go to

14

the old man's right hand, that he may bless you." But when Brother Elias placed himself at his right hand, Saint Francis, who was unable to see through much weeping, and had placed his right hand on his head, said: "This is not the head of my firstborn, Brother Bernard." Then Brother Bernard came to his left hand. But Saint Francis crossed his arms, and changing over hands, placed his left hand on the head of Brother Elias and his right on Brother Bernard, saying to the latter: "The Father of my Lord Jesus Christ bless you with every spiritual blessing in the heavenly places in Christ. Just as you were the first chosen in this Order to give an evangelical example and imitate Christ in evangelical poverty, and, in generosity, gave to the poor all you had for love of Christ, but even offered up your person as a sweet smelling sacrifice to God, so may you be blessed by the Lord Jesus Christ and by me, his poor little servant, with eternal blessings at your going out and coming in, waking and sleeping, living and dying. Let whoever blesses you be filled with blessings, and whoever speaks ill of you shall not go unscathed. Be the master of your brethren and let them be subject to your authority. Whoever you wish to be received into this Order, let him be received, and whoever you wish to be expelled, let it so be. And let no brother hold authority over you and may you be free to go and stay as you will."

When that blessed Friar drew near to death, whom the brethren, after Saint Francis's passing, revered with love like to a father, many came to see him from different places. Among them was the holy leader, the holy Brother Giles. Beholding Brother Bernard, he said to him with great joy: "Lift up your heart, Brother Bernard, lift up your heart." Brother Bernard told one of the brethren quietly to prepare a place suitable for contemplation, where Brother Giles could think about heavenly things.

When Brother Bernard reached the final hour of his departure, he had them sit him up, and to the brethren standing round he said: "Dearest brethren, I do not wish to say much to you, but you should bear in mind that my condition now will be yours some day, just as you hold the same vocation. I found in my soul that I would not have renounced the service of Christ for a thousand worlds like this. For every sin I have committed, I accuse myself before my Savior Jesus Christ and you. I beg you, dearest brethren, love one another." After these words and other profitable exhortations, he lay back on his bed, and his face shone with a great joy, astonishing to all about him. And in that happiness that joyous soul, with the victory before promised him, passed to the joys of the blessed. To the praise of God.

Chapter 6

The lenten fast of Saint Francis.

FRANCIS, TRUEST SERVANT OF CHRIST, was in many ways like a second Christ given to the world. God therefore made that happy man in many ways like his son Jesus Christ. That was obvious in the sacred society of his companions, in the wondrous mystery of the sacred Stigmata of the Cross, and in his holy lenten fast. For once when he was near Lake Trasimene on Carnival Day, he was the guest of a man devoted to him. He asked him for God's love to take him secretly to an island in the lake where no one lived, on the eve of Ash Wednesday. For the great reverence in which he held Saint Francis he zealously did so. Getting ready his little boat on Ash Wednesday, he ferried him over. Saint Francis had no food with him but two small loaves.

Set ashore on the island, he asked his ferryman not to reveal this to anyone, and to come to him on Holy Thursday. Since there was no building where to lay his head, he crawled into a dense thicket where the vines made a kind of shelter, and stayed there through the whole forty days, without eating or drinking.

The host, according to their agreement, sought him on Holy Thursday and found, save for half of one loaf, the rest was not touched. It is believed that Saint Francis touched that one half, that the glory of the forty-day fast should be reserved for the blessed Christ, that by that small loaf the poison of vainglory should be driven out, though he had fasted after Christ's example forty days and forty nights. Afterwards, in that same place where Saint Francis had demonstrated such endurance, many miracles were done through his merits, so that people began to build and live there on that island and it came about that, after a short lapse of time, a considerable village and a friary of the friars minor emerged. So it came about that the folk of that village show great reverence for the place where Saint Francis kept Lent. Glory be to God.

Chapter 7

The lesson of Saint Francis to Brother Leo—only in the Cross is there perfect happiness.

ON A WINTER DAY Saint Francis was journeying from Perugia to Saint Mary of the Angels. Brother Leo was with him and the bitter cold tormented both of them. Saint Francis called out to Brother Leo who was a short distance in front: "Brother Leo, though the friars minor are setting a high example of holiness and uprightness and good edification, yet write down and note well that therein is not perfect happiness." A little further on, he called to him again: "Brother Leo, though a friar minor give sight to the blind and straighten a twisted body, drive out demons, give hearing to the deaf, make the lame walk and the dumb speak, and even raise the four days dead, write down that this is not perfect happiness." And, again, he loudly called: "Brother Leo, though a friar minor should know the speech of all peoples, all sciences and Scriptures, and how to prophesy, and show not only what is yet to be, but even what lies in the heart of others, write down that this is not perfect happiness." A little further on, as they were still walking, he called out once more: "Brother Leo, little lamb of God, though a friar minor speak with the tongue of angels, know the courses of the stars, the virtues of herbs, and the secret of earth's treasure, and understand the qualities and peculiarities of fish, beasts, men, roots, trees, stones and waters, write down clearly, and carefully note, that this is not perfect happiness." And after a little while he called again: "Brother Leo, though a friar minor should know how so earnestly to preach that he should bring all unbelievers to faith, write that here is not perfect happiness."

So the conversation continued for two miles. But Brother Leo, very baffled by all this, said: "Father, I beg you in God's name, tell me where lies perfect happiness?" The saint replied: "We shall come to Saint Mary of the Angels thus drenched in rain, stiff with cold, defiled with mud and afflicted with hunger, and knock at the door; and if the porter comes angrily and asks: "Who are you?" we reply: "We are two of your Brethren." And if he should contradict and answer: "No, you are a pair of vagrants who go about everywhere, seizing on the alms of the poor," and should not open to us, but make us stand in the snow

18

and rain, cold and hungry until night; and if then we patiently endure submissively and without complaint to much wrong and rejection, humbly and charitably thinking that the porter truly recognizes us, and that God stirs his tongue against us, then Brother Leo, write down that there lies perfect happiness. And if we continue knocking, and the porter comes out angry at our persistence, and cruelly heaps blows on us saying: "Be off, basest rogues, go to the poorhouse. Who are you? Certainly you shall not eat here." And if we endure patiently and accept his abuse with love wholehearted, Brother Leo, write that there lies perfect happiness. And if we in all ways afflicted, with hunger pressing, cold tormenting us, and night approaching, go on knocking, calling and pleading with tears that he should open to us, and he, stirred thus, should say: "These are persistent trouble-makers. I will deal with them," and coming out with a knotted cudgel, and seizing us by the hood he will fling us down in the mud and snow, battering us all over with his cudgel—if we bear such ills and abuse with joy, bearing in mind the sufferings of the blessed Christ which we must both bear with the utmost patience, consider Brother Leo, among all the gifts of the Holy Spirit which Christ offered and still does to those who love him, this is to conquer self for Christ's sake and by the love of God gladly to suffer shame, this is happiness. We cannot glory in any gifts of God than these, because they are his, not ours. For the Apostle says: "What have you that you did not receive? If you did receive, what have you to boast about, as if you had not received?"—But in the Cross of suffering and trouble we may indeed glory, because this is our part. That is why the Apostle said: "Far be it from me to glory except in the Cross of our Lord."

Chapter 8

Brother Leo's godlike talk to Saint Francis.

SAINT FRANCIS, IN THE EARLY DAYS of the Order, was in a small village with Brother Leo where they had no books from which to say mass. One night, when they had risen for matins, Saint Francis said to his colleague: "Dearest man, we have no breviary from which to recite matins: but that we may spend our time in the praise of God, so speak as I shall bid you, and be careful not to alter the words in any way. I shall speak as follows: 'Brother Francis, you have committed so many sins in the world that you deserve hell.' And you, Brother Leo, reply: 'True it is that you have deserved hell.'" Brother Leo, that most blameless man, with the simplicity of a dove, replied: "Gladly, Father. Begin in the name of the Lord." And Saint Francis began to say, as he had said he would, "O Brother Francis, you have committed so many sins in this world that you deserve hell." And Brother Leo replied: "God will do so much good through you that you will go to paradise." But Saint Francis said: "Do not speak thus, Brother Leo, but when I say: 'O Brother Francis, you have done so many evil deeds contrary to God's will that you deserve to be accursed,' then do you reply: 'You deserve to be counted among the accursed.'" And Brother Leo said: "Gladly, Father."

Then Saint Francis, with many tears, sighs and beatings of his breast and crying aloud, said: "Lord, God of heaven and of earth, I have committed so many dire sins against you, that I deserve to be utterly damned." But Brother Leo answered: "God will so

20

ordain that amid the blessed you shall be uncommonly blessed." And Saint Francis, surprised that his reply was always contradictory, rebuking him, said: "Why, Brother Leo, do you not reply as I instruct you? In holy obedience, I direct you to reply in accordance with the words I use to you. I shall say this: 'Brother Francis, worthless fellow, do you think that God will have mercy on you when you have committed so many sins against the Father of mercies, and the God of all consolation that you are not worthy of pardon?' And you, brother lamb, must reply: 'In no way are you worthy of finding mercy.' " And Brother Leo replied: "God the Father whose mercy is infinitely greater than your sins, will show you great mercy and add thereto manifold grace."

But Saint Francis was somewhat put out and a little upset. He said, "Why, brother, did you presume, contrary to your obedience, and so often answer contrary to my directions?" Then Brother Leo replied reverently and most humbly: "God knows, dearest father, that I always set out to do as you order, but God made me speak as I did." Saint Francis was very amazed at this, and said to Brother Leo: "I beg you, in deepest love, to answer me this time as I have told you." "Speak, in God's name," said Brother Leo, "and I will." And Saint Francis in tears said: "Brother Francis, miserable little wretch, do you think that God will have mercy on you?" Brother Leo answered: "You will receive grace from God, great grace indeed from him who exalts the humble. I cannot speak in any other way for God is speaking through my mouth." And in this duel of humility they continued awake together until dawn. To the praise and glory of our Lord Jesus Christ. Amen.

Chapter 9

The discovery of Mount Alverna and Brother Leo's vision concerning Saint Francis.

THAT MOST FAITHFUL SERVANT and friend of Jesus Christ, Saint Francis, honored the Creator and his Savior with all his might, both through his own efforts and through others. The most gracious and benign Savior Jesus repaid him the honor for "Whosoever glorifies me, him will I glorify," saith the Lord. and so wherever Saint Francis went he was held in such veneration that practically everybody flocked to such a wonderful man. Wherever he went—country, castle or country houses—whoever managed to touch or see him considered himself blessed.

It happened on one occasion, before he received the Savior's stigmata, that returning from the valley of Spoleto he was proceeding to Romagna. As he reached the castle of Monte Feltro, there was being celebrated a great ceremony of knighting. When the holy father heard of this from the local inhabitants he said to his companion Brother Leo: "Let us go there, for with God's help we shall make some progress among them." Attending the ceremony were many nobles from various places, among them a certain lord from Tuscany, by name Orlando, a very rich nobleman who because of the wonderful things he had heard about Saint Francis, had conceived a great devotion for him and desired to see and hear him. Saint Francis entering the castle mounted up on to a parapet, the more conveniently to be heard by the multitude, and there preached to them. For his subject he announced in the vernacular: "Tanto e il bene ch'io aspetto, ch'ogni pena m'e diletto," meaning, so great is the good that I expect, that any pain is a pleasure. And on this subject the Holy Spirit poured forth out of his mouth such devout and godly eloquence, substantiating it with the sufferings of the martyrs, the martyrdom of the apostles, the grievous penance of those who confessed their sins, the frequent tribulations of saintly men and women, that all stood enthralled as if listening to an angel. Among them was the lord Orlando aforesaid, rejoicing greatly in the presence of Saint Francis that he had prayed for, inwardly moved by his wonderful preaching, and very eager to discuss the salvation of his soul with the holy father. And so when the sermon was over he said to Saint Francis: "Father, I should like to discuss with you certain matters concerning the salvation of my soul." Saint Francis, full seasoned with the salt of discretion, said to him: "My lord, this morning go and pay your respects to your friends since you are their guest at this celebration; after dinner we shall talk as long as you wish." He agreed, and after dinner discoursed at great length with Saint Francis on the salvation of his soul. Finally he said: "Brother Francis, in Tuscany I possess at Alverna a very sacred and very solitary mountain called Mount Alverna, very suitable for those who desire to live a solitary life. If this mountain were to the taste of your companions I would very gladly present it to you for the salvation of my soul."

Saint Francis desired very sincerely to find solitary places where he could more conveniently devote himself to divine contemplation. When he heard this offer he first gave thanks to God who provides for his sheep through the medium of his faithful followers, then thanking lord Orlando he replied thus: "My Lord, when you have returned to your estates I shall send to you two of my companions, and you shall show them this mountain, and if it seems suitable I shall most gladly accept your generous offer." The said lord lived in his own castle near Mount Alverna.

And so when the celebration was over and the lord had returned home to his castle, Saint Francis sent two of his companions to seek him out; but owing to their unfamiliarity with those parts, they had great difficulty in finding the castle. When they did find him they were welcomed with affection and great joy as if they were angels of God. Escorted by fifty armed men for fear of danger from wild beasts, they were conducted to the said Mount Alverna. Here seeking a spot where they could prepare a place to live they finally discovered a small level area where in God's name they proposed to stay. The laymen who accompanied the friars cut down branches from the trees with their swords and with them built a kind of hut. Having taken possession of the spot they departed, affirming in the name of Saint Francis that it was extremely remote and suitable for contemplation. Saint Francis on hearing this gave praise to God, and taking with him Brother Masseo, Brother Leo and Brother Angelo, a former soldier, made his way with them to the mountain. During the ascent with his blessed companions, as they rested a little while under an oak tree, a flock of birds of various kinds descended upon Saint Francis with joyous song and fluttering wings. Some settled on his head, some on his shoulders, some on his knees, some on the hands of the holy father. At such a strange and wonderful sight Saint Francis said to his companions: "I believe, my very beloved brethren, that it is the will of our Lord Jesus Christ, that we should occupy a place on this lonely mountain where our sisters the birds show such joy at our coming." And rising up rejoicing greatly in spirit, he continued on to the afore-said spot where there was still nothing but that very lowly hut made from branches of trees. Having sought out a lonely spot where he could pray away from the others, he built a very modest cell on the mountain side and gave orders that none of his companions should come near him; nor should allow any one else to approach except Brother Leo, for there he intended to observe the fast in honor of the archangel Michael. Even Brother Leo he instructed to come to him only once a day bringing bread and water, and once during the night at the hour of matins. Then he was to approach in silence quoting only: "Lord, open thou my lips" and if he replied from within: "And my mouth shall show forth thy praise" they were to say matins together. But if he did not respond immediately Brother Leo was to withdraw. He gave this order because he was sometimes in such a state of ecstasy that for whole days and nights he was unable to speak, being thus absorbed in God. This order Brother Leo observed very punctiliously. Nevertheless, as unobtrusively as possible he tried to find out what the saint was doing. Sometimes he would find him outside the cell elevated in the air so that he could touch his feet. Then he would clasp his feet and cover them with tearful kisses saying: "God be merciful to me a sinner, and grant that through the merits of this holy man I may obtain mercy." On one occasion he found him elevated to half the height of a beech tree that grew to such a lofty height. On another occasion he found him elevated from the ground to such a height that he could scarcely see him. Brother Leo would then genuflect and stretch at full length on the ground from which the holy father, still praying, was raised aloft. And Brother Leo himself would pray, and commending himself to God as before through the merits of the holy father, would experience the full impact of divine grace. And thanks to all the saint's experiences that he had so often observed, Brother Leo was now possessed of such devotion to him that very frequently, by day or by night, he scrutinized with divine perception the mysterious preoccupations of Saint Francis. And so it fell out that during the aforementioned fast, he once went to seek out Saint Francis as was his custom, to say matins. As soon as he entered he said: "Lord, open thou my lips" as he had been instructed to do. There was no answer, and by the light of the moon he perceived that the saint was not in his cell. While he pondered what prayer to say, peering through the wood this way and that, he heard him speaking. Drawing near in order to hear what he was saying, by the light of the moon he saw the saint on bended knees, his face raised to heaven, hands outstretched to God saying: "What art thou, sweetest God, and what am I, a mere worm and thy insignificant slave?" These words, and nothing else, he kept repeating. And as he gazed Brother Leo beheld descending from the heights of the heavens onto the head of Saint Francis a most beauteous fiery flame, exceedingly bright and a delight to the eyes. And from this flame came forth a voice speaking to Saint Francis, to which he kept replying.

But in order not to intrude upon the saint in such holy privacy Brother Leo drew back and concealed himself so as not to hear what was being said. But he did see that three times Saint Francis held out his hand towards the flame. As the flame receded Brother Leo began to withdraw completely in order not to be perceived by the saint. But Saint Francis hearing the sound of his feet stumbling over some branch or other said: "I command thee, whosoever thou art, by the authority of our Lord Jesus Christ, to stand still. Do not move from the spot." Immediately in response to the saint's adjuration he stood still and said: "It is I, father." Brother Leo subsequently related that he was so petrified with fear, that if the earth had opened he would cheerfully have hid himself therein. For he feared that if he offended the saint he would forfeit the favor of his company. For such was the trust and affection he had for the saint that he had no confidence whatever in life without him. This was why whenever people talked about saints Brother Leo would say: "Dear friends, all saints are great, yes; but in fact Saint Francis belongs to the great because of the miracles that God works through him." Acknowledging his word the saint said: "Brother sheep of the flock, is this why you came here? How many times have I not told you not to go about watching what I do? Tell me, by your vow of obedience, what did you see?" He answered: "Father, I heard you talking, speaking and frequently praying in great awe, 'What art thou sweetest God, and what am I but a mere worm and thy humble slave.' And then I beheld a flame descending from heaven and speaking with you; and I saw you answer several times and hold out your hand, but what you said I know not." Genuflecting with great respect Brother Leo asked the saint: "I beg you, Father, explain to me the words I heard, and tell me the ones I did not hear." And Saint Francis full of affection for Brother Leo because of his sincerity and gentleness said: "O brother sheep of the flock of Jesus Christ, in what you saw and heard were revealed to me two lights, one concerning the knowledge of the Creator, and the other concerning myself. When I said: 'What art thou, Lord my God, and who am I?' then I was bathed in rays of contemplation in which I saw the extent of the infiniteness of God, and the deplorable depths of my vileness. That is why I kept saying: 'Why is it Lord, all highest, wise, supremely good and supremely merciful, that thou visitest me, who am supremely vile, a miserable, abominable and contemptible worm?' Indeed that was God speaking to me in that guise just as he spoke to Moses in the burning bush. Among other things God asked me to make him three gifts. I replied: 'All I have is a habit, a girdle and breeches; and even those too are really thine. What then shall I be able to offer thy mighty majesty? For heaven and earth, fire and water, and all that is in them are thine, O Lord. For who possesses anything that is not thine? Therefore when we offer thee anything we render to thee what is thine. What then can I offer thee, Lord God of heaven and earth and all creation?' And God said to me: 'Put your hand in your bosom

27

and offer me whatever you find there.' When I did so I found a golden coin so great, brilliant and beautiful, such as I had never seen in this world, and this I offered to God. Again God said: 'Make me another offering as before.' But I said: 'Lord, I have nothing, love nothing, desire nothing except thee; for thy sake I have rejected gold and all things else. And so if anything else is found in my bosom, thou didst place it there, and to thee I make restitution, O Lord of all.' And this I did three times. After the third offering I genuflected and blessed God who gave me the wherewithal to make an offering. And forthwith it was granted to me to understand what that threefold offering represented: golden obedience, most abject poverty, and admirable chastity, that God by his favor gave to me to be so perfectly observed that in nothing did my conscience reproach me. Then just as each time I thrust my hand into my bosom I brought forth and gave back those coins to the same God who had placed them there, so did God grant me the power in my soul ever to praise God and magnify him with heart and voice for all the blessings which in his holy goodness he has bestowed on me. This then was the meaning of the words you heard and the outstretching of my hands that you saw. Therefore, brother sheep, beware, do not go about watching me; return to your cell with God's blessing, and be assiduous in taking care of me. For within a few days God will work such amazing miracles on this mountain that the whole world will be filled with wonder. For he will do strange things that he has never done in this world to any creature." So Brother Leo withdrew greatly comforted. Indeed during that same lenten fast there appeared on that very mountain, at about the season of the Exaltation of the Holy Cross, Christ in the shape of a winged seraph, and as if crucified, imprinting both the nails and the stigmata on the hands, feet and side of Saint Francis as his legend relates. And he appeared at night with such brilliance that he lit up the various mountains and valleys round about more brightly than if it had been the light of the sun. Witnesses of this were shepherds in those parts watching with their flocks.

Why the sacred stigmata were imprinted on Saint Francis has not been revealed to everybody. But just as he himself used to tell the story to his companions, so this great mystery is carried on into the future.

This story Brother James of Massa had from the mouth of Brother Leo, and Brother Ugolino of Monte Santa Maria from the mouth of the said Brother James; and I, the present writer who have recorded it, had it from the mouth of Brother Ugolino, a man in every respect trustworthy. To the praise of God.

Chapter 10

How Brother Masseo examined the humility of Saint Francis.

SAINT FRANCIS WAS STAYING on one occasion at the friary of the Porziuncula along with Brother Masseo, who spoke of God with singular grace and understanding. That is why he was loved by the saint. Once when Saint Francis came in from the wood where he had been to pray, and was about to leave the shelter of the trees, Brother Masseo meeting him, and wishing to try out how humble he was, said : "Why you? Why you? Why you?" Saint Francis replied: "What do you mean, Brother Masseo?" He replied: "The whole world seems to go after you, all seek to see you, to hear you, to obey you, but you are not a handsome man. You are not a man of great knowledge or wisdom. You are not noble. Why, therefore, does the whole world come to you?" When the blessed Francis heard this, he

29

rejoiced in spirit, and lifting his face to heaven stood for a long time, his mind turned to God. He came to himself, fell on his knees, and with praise and thanks to God with great warmth of spirit, turned to Brother Masseo and said: "You wish to know why me, why me, why me. You wish to know, and know truly, why the whole world comes after me. This comes to me from those most holy eyes of God which everywhere observe both good and evil. Those blessed and most holy eyes saw among evil men no greater sinner, more useless and vile than me. Therefore to do the wondrous work he had in mind to do, since he could find on earth no one more vile, he chose me, for God has chosen the foolish things of the world to confound the wise, the mean, contemptible, feeble things of the world to confound the noble and the great, so that the grandeur of goodness should proceed from God, and not from that which God has created, so that no creature and no flesh should boast in his sight, and that to God alone should be honor and glory for ever."

Then Brother Masseo was amazed at a reply so humble and so warmly made, and truly knew that the holy father was grounded in true humility, a true and humble follower of Christ.

Chapter 11

How Saint Francis realized what Brother Masseo concealed in his heart.

ONCE IN TUSCANY, Saint Francis was on the road with Brother Masseo whom, for his grace of speech and singular discretion, he most gladly took along with him. He was a help, too, when the saint was in a state of rapture, by dealing with visitors and hiding him from them. When one day they were thus journeying, Brother Masseo was going ahead of Saint Francis over a section of the journey. When they came to a place where three roads met (one to Sienna, one to Florence, one to Arezzo), Brother Masseo said: "Father, which road must we take?" The saint replied: "We must take the road God wills." Brother Masseo said: "And how shall we discover the will of God?" The saint replied: "By the sign I shall show in you. In the name of your holy obedience I bid you, in the crossways where now you stand, that you turn round and round as children do, and do not stop turning until I tell you."

Like a true and obedient man, he twirled round there so long that from the giddiness of head which such turning brings on, he kept falling down. But since the saint did not tell him to stop he obediently got up and resumed his turning. Then said Saint Francis: "In which direction is your face turned?" He replied: "To Sienna." The saint said: "That is the way God wishes us to go." Brother Masseo was very amazed at the childish things he had made him do, twirling thus before many who passed by, but for reverence' sake he did not dare to say anything to the holy father. But when they drew near Sienna and the city people knew about the holy father's arrival they came out to meet him and carried both of them to the bishop's house so that they hardly put foot to ground the whole way.

At that time some citizens of Sienna were in conflict with one another and already two had been killed. But Saint Francis arose and pleaded with them so graciously, and in such holy fashion, that he brought them all to peace and great concord. Hearing of so wonderful a deed, the bishop of Sienna took Saint Francis in and entertained him with great honor. Early the next morning, however, Saint Francis, in true humility, seeking in all he did nothing but God's glory, rose betimes with his companions and they went away without a word to the bishop.

So Brother Masseo said to himself as they journeyed: "What has this good man done? Yesterday he made me twirl round like a child, and today he says not a good word nor returns thanks to a bishop who has so honored him." It all seemed to him unwise. Later, at the urging of God, he thought over it again and reproached himself in his heart, saying: "Brother Masseo, you are overproud, you who so judge the works of God are worthy of hell for rebelling against God in your unwise arrogance, for on this journey such holy works have been done by Saint Francis, that, if an angel of God had done them, it would not have been more wonderful. So, if he ordered you to throw stones you ought to obey him. All the things he did on this journey proceeded from the ordinance of God, as appears from the successful outcome. Unless those combatants had been brought to peace, not only would the sword have eaten up the bodies of more men, as it had begun to do, but, worse, the gulf of hell would have devoured, with the Devil's aid, the souls of many more. And that is why you are a very arrogant fool for grumbling about what is manifestly the will of God."

So Brother Masseo was saying in his heart, as he walked a little ahead of Saint Francis.

But Saint Francis, by God's Spirit, was made aware of this, for to him all things are naked and open. He called out behind Brother Masseo's back, and said, revealing the hidden things of his heart: "Hold fast to those things you are now thinking, for they are good, profitable and inspired by God. Your first murmurings were blind, bad, and proud, sown in your soul by the Devil." Hearing this Brother Masseo was amazed. Saint Francis obviously knew the secrets of his heart, and above all else he understood that the Spirit of divine grace guided Saint Francis in all he did. To the praise and glory of our Lord Jesus Christ. Amen.

Chapter 12

How Brother Masseo was tested by Saint Francis.

OUR MOST BLESSED FATHER FRANCIS, wishing to teach Brother Masseo humility so that the manifold gifts the Most High had given him should increase the more, when the holy father was in retreat with his first truly holy companions, including Brother Masseo, said before the whole group: "Brother Masseo, all of these your companions have the grace of prayer and contemplation, but you have the grace of the Word of God to meet the needs of visitors. That is why, in order that they may be more free for prayer and contemplation, I wish you to be doorkeeper, almoner and have charge of the kitchen. When the brothers are at table you will eat outside the door so that, before visitors knock, you may satisfy them with a few words, so that no one need go outside but you. Do this in the name of sanctified obedience."

At this Brother Masseo immediately bowed his head and drew back his cowl and humbly obeyed. For several days he kept watch over door, alms and kitchen. But his companions, like men enlightened by God, became conscious of much inner strife of heart, because Brother Masseo was a man of great perfection and prayer as they were and more so, and yet the whole burden of the friary had been laid on him. So they asked the holy father to share out the duties among them for in no way could their consciences endure that the said brother should bear so many burdens. Further, they felt ineffectual in their prayers, and troubled in conscience unless Brother Masseo should be eased of his burdens.

Saint Francis, hearing this, agreed to the loving suggestions. He called Brother Masseo and said: "Brother Masseo, these your companions wish to take a share of the duties I have laid on you. I therefore wish the duties to be shared out." He humbly and patiently replied: "Father, whatever wholly or in part you lay upon me, I wholly consider it to be an act of God."

Then Saint Francis, observing their love and Brother Masseo's humility, gave a most wondrous sermon on holy humility, apart from which no virtue is acceptable in the eyes of God. He then shared out the duties and blessed all of them with the grace of the Holy Spirit. To the praise of God.

Chapter 13

How Saint Francis elevated Brother Masseo in the air with his breath.

THAT WONDROUS SERVANT OF GOD and true disciple of Christ, Saint Francis, in order to be like Christ in everything, just as Christ sent his disciples out two by two to every community and friary where he was to come himself, so, after gathering a company of twelve, he dispersed them in pairs to preach everywhere. To show an example of true obedience in himself, he himself first, like Christ, began rather to do than teach. So, having sent his companions in various directions, choosing Brother Masseo for companion, he took the road to France.

When they reached one hamlet, where out of necessity as the Rule directs, they had to beg, Brother Francis went along one street and Brother Masseo along another. Saint Francis because, as a small-built man, and therefore, after human fashion almost universally despised among strangers, received a few bits of old bread and small crusts; but more and better bread was given to Brother Masseo because he was a fine looking man and tall in stature. When they met they found a spring on the edge of which was a wide beautiful stone. They rejoiced greatly and on the stone placed the bits of bread they had acquired. And when Saint Francis saw that the pieces of bread which Brother Masseo had acquired were more and better than his, rejoicing in spirit because of his longing for poverty, he said: "Brother Masseo, we are undeserving of such great treasure." He said this again and again, in a louder and louder voice. Brother Masseo answered: "Dearest father, how can this be called treasure where there is such poverty, no tablecloth, no knife, bowl, trencher, house, table, man servant nor maid?" Saint Francis replied: "That is what I call great treasure, where nothing has been provided by man's labor. All else has been provided by God's providence, as appears manifest in the bread we have, in so beauteous a stone, and so limpid a spring. So I want us to pray to God begging that he will make us wholeheartedly love the noble treasure of holy poverty supplied by God."

From those crusts of bread, the spring, the food and drink consumed with godly song, they rose to continue on their road to France. They arrived at a church, went in, and Saint Francis hid behind the altar to pray. There he experienced such exceeding fire of divine revelation, his soul was so utterly set on fire with a desire for poverty that he seemed to emit from face and breath as it were flames of love. Coming out to his companion with such fiery breath he exclaimed:

"A, a, a, a, Brother Masseo, surrender to me." This he said three times. Amazed at such fervor, at the third invocation Masseo flung himself into the holy father's arms. Saint Francis, with a deep breath, and the heat of the Holy Spirit, shouted loudly "A, a, a, a," and lifted Brother Masseo into the air with his very breathing, and impelled him along before him for the length of a long spear. Before such a wondrous manifestation of the Holy Spirit's warmth, Brother Masseo was amazed, and later confessed to his companions that as he was lifted and driven along by Saint Francis he experienced such sweetness and comfort of the Holy Spirit that never in his life had he sensed anything so wondrous.

Then said Saint Francis to Brother Masseo: "Let us now go to Rome to Saint Peter and Saint Paul, and ask them to teach us and enable us to lay hold of the unutterable treasure of holy poverty." He continued: "Dearest and most beloved brother, the treasure of blessed poverty is so surpassingly worthy and so divine that we are not worthy to contain it in these utterly vile vessels, for poverty is that heavenly virtue by which the things of earth and time are all trodden underfoot, by which all obstacles are removed, and the human mind is freely joined with God Eternal. This, too, is what makes it possible for a soul on earth to converse with the angels of heaven. This is what went with Christ to the Cross, was hidden with Christ in the tomb, rose with him and ascended to heaven, for this virtue grants the gift, even in this life, to those souls who love her, of flying to heaven. She alone guards the armor of humility and love. So let us pray the most holy apostles of Christ who loved this pearl of the Gospel, to obtain this grace for us from the Lord Jesus Christ, that he, the practicer and teacher of holy poverty, may deign, in his most holy mercy, to grant to us that we may deserve to be true practicers and humble disciples of the most precious, lovable and evangelical poverty."

Reaching Rome, they went into the Church of Saint Peter. Saint Francis went to one corner of that church and Brother Masseo to another to pray to God and his holy apostles that they would instruct them and help them to lay hold of the treasure of holy poverty. For this they asked with deep devotion and many tears. But as they continued in such humble prayer, behold the blessed Peter and the blessed Paul appeared in great splendor to Saint Francis. They kissed him, embraced him and said: "Father Francis, since you seek and long for what Christ himself and his holy apostles served, we bring you word from the Lord Jesus Christ that your desire is granted. The Lord Jesus Christ himself has sent us to tell you that your prayer is heard, and the treasure of divinest poverty is granted you and your followers. And to you we say, at Christ's behest, that whoever pursues this desire after your perfect example shall be assured of the kingdom of blessedness, and you and all who follow you shall be blessed of God."

This said, they disappeared leaving him deeply comforted. Saint Francis, rising from prayer, went to his companion and asked him whether he had had anything from God. He replied that he had had nothing. But Saint Francis told how the holy apostles had appeared to him and revealed what has just been told. At this both were filled with such joy and happiness that, forgetting their intended visit to France, they hastily returned to the valley of Spoleto, where this heavenly and angelic journey was to begin.

Chapter 14

How Christ appeared in the midst of his companions as Saint Francis spoke to them about God.

OUR VERY HOLY FATHER FRANCIS, who directed all his thoughts towards the blessed Christ, and directed all his zeal and longing for prayer and speech to his good will for himself and his companions, was once sitting with them, his blessed children, soon after his conversion. In fervor of spirit he bade one of them open his mouth in the name of the Lord, and speak to God in such way as the Holy Spirit suggested. When he obediently began, and as the spirit prompted was uttering amazing words, the blessed father imposed silence on him, and bade a second brother likewise to speak of God according to the grace given him by the Holy Spirit. He obeyed and by the grace of God was pouring out wondrous words about God when Saint Francis imposed silence upon him as he had upon the first. And he imposed upon a third the task of uttering something to the praise of the Lord Jesus Christ without premeditation. The third, like the other two, fulfilling humbly his obedience, brought to light such marvellous and secret things about the hidden things of God, that there was no doubt that through him, as through the rest, the Holy Spirit was speaking.

So when, one by one, those vessels of holy simple men were pouring out the balm of God's grace, like the honey of God flowing by the holy father's command, behold, in the guise of a most handsome youth, the Lord Jesus Christ appeared among them, blessing them all with such sweetness of grace, that the holy father, and all the rest, were enraptured, and lay on the ground as though dead to this world, feeling nothing. When they recovered consciousness, the holy father said: "Dearest brethren, give thanks to the Lord Jesus Christ, because he was pleased to spread the treasures of heaven through the lips of simple men. He who opened the mouth of infants and of the dumb, makes the tongues of the simple, when he so wishes, most wise and eloquent." To the glory of God.

Chapter 15

How Saint Francis and his companions were rapt together with Saint Clare.

FRANCIS, SERVANT OF GOD MOST HIGH, often in his lifetime gave consolation to the most blessed Clare. She asked the blessed Father Francis to grant her this consolation, to wit, to have one meal together. The blessed Father Francis always refused to do so. So it came about that the companions of the holy father, considering the wish of the holy Clare, said to the blessed Francis: "Father, it seems to us that this determination is not according to the love of God, not to listen to Sister Clare, a virgin so holy and beloved of God, especially since it was under your preaching that she abandoned the pomp of the world. And so you do not agree to take even one meal with her; if with such insistence she had asked for a greater favor, you would have had to grant it as to a spiritual plant of your own." Saint Francis replied: "You think I should hearken to this request?" They said: "Yes, Father, for she is worthy of this comfort from you." Saint Francis replied: "Since this is what you think good, so too it seems good to me; but that the comfort may be yet greater, let it be at Saint Mary of the Angels. She has long been cloistered in the church of Saint Damian and she will take some small joy in seeing again the shrine of Saint Mary where her hair was cut and she became the bride of Jesus Christ the Lord. There we shall eat together in the name of the Lord."

So he fixed a day on which the most blessed Clare should come with one other nun, he being accompanied by his companions. She came and after reverent and humble adoration of Mary, the Mother of the Lord, and a devout inspection of the place, came the time appointed for the meal. The humble and godly Francis had the table prepared, as was his custom, on the bare ground. He and the blessed Clare took their places, as did one of the holy Father's companions with the companion of the holy Clare. All of the other of Francis's companions also took their places at the humble table. As the first dish was set before them, Saint Francis began to speak of God in so sweet, holy, lofty and divine a way, that Saint Francis himself, Saint Clare and her companion, and all who were at that modest little table, were caught up in mighty and abundant grace from the Most High that came upon them.

As they were thus sitting in ecstasy and lifting eyes and hands to heaven, the people of Assisi and Bettona and all along the road thought that the whole of Saint Mary of the Angels, the building, and the wood which then surrounded it, were on fire, and an enormous conflagration enveloped the whole. So the men of Assisi ran hastily to save the building, firmly convinced it would burn down completely. When they arrived they found it all unharmed and intact. Going in they found Saint Francis, Saint Clare, and all their company in a divine ecstasy, all sitting at that most humble table, and clothed with virtue from on high. And of a certainty they knew that it was the fire of God

40

which blazed about those saintly folk, and went away uplifted and comforted.

So refreshed were Saint Francis, Saint Clare and their company by so rich a comfort from God in their soul, that they touched little or nothing of the corporeal food before them. Saint Clare went back to Saint Damian's church and the sisters rejoiced to see her, for they feared Saint Francis might wish to send her to be head of another nunnery, as he had sent her sister Agnes to Florence as abbess, and had once said to Saint Clare: "Be prepared if need be to go wherever I shall send you." And like a truly obedient daughter, she had replied: "I am ready, father, to go wherever you wish." So Saint Clare stayed on, deeply comforted in the Lord.

Chapter 16

**How God revealed to Saint Clare and
Brother Silvester that Saint Francis was destined
to go out and preach.**

IN THE EARLY DAYS after his conversion, when he had already gathered several companions round him, Saint Francis found himself in a position of agonizing doubt as to whether he should keep himself free for uninterrupted prayer, or should give his energies at times to preaching. He had a great desire to know the will and good pleasure of our Lord Jesus Christ on this matter. Holy humility would not permit him to trust himself, so he humbly turned to the refuge others could offer, by whose prayers he was able to recognize the divine good pleasure in this matter. So he called Brother Masseo, and said to him: "Dearest man, go to Sister Clare and say to her on my behalf that she must, along with one of the purest and most spiritual of her sisters, ask God in prayer, and tell me what she thinks best, whether I should occasionally preach, or give myself to uninterrupted prayer. Go also to Brother Silvester, who lives on Mount Subasio and similarly ask him." That Brother Silvester was of such holiness and grace that whatever he sought in prayer was immediately answered. The Holy Spirit had made him especially worthy of converse with God. That is why Saint Francis had great trust and faith in him. Brother Silvester lived as a hermit on Mount Subasio already mentioned.

Brother Masseo following his orders from Saint Francis, went first to the blessed Clare and then to Brother Silvester and gave the message. Brother Silvester immediately proceeded to prayer and forthwith had God's answer. He went out to Brother Masseo and said: "The Lord thus directs that you should reply to Brother Francis, that God called him not for himself alone, but for a harvest of souls, and that he should bless many through him." After this Brother Masseo went back to the holy Clare to find whether she had anything from God. She replied that both she and her companion had from God a reply altogether like that of Brother Silvester.

Brother Masseo came back to Saint Francis who received him with love, washing his feet and preparing a meal. After the meal he called him into the wood. He bared his head, crossed his arms, fell on his knees and asked: "What does my Lord Jesus Christ bid me do?" Brother Masseo reported the reply of the blessed Jesus Christ as it came through Brother Silvester, Sister Clare and her companion, to wit, that it was his will "that you continue with preaching, because God called you not for your sake alone but for the salvation of others." Then it was clear that the hand of God was upon Saint Francis. Rising in fervor of spirit, all afire with the virtue of the Most High, he said to Brother Masseo: "Let us then go, in the Lord's name."

Taking as his companions Brother Masseo himself and Brother Angelo, both holy men, he set out like a lightning flash in the drive of the Spirit. With no thought for road or path they came to the fortress of Cannara where he preached with great fervor. Because of this and the miracle of the twittering swallows who fell silent at his command, every man and woman in that place wished to leave home and follow him. But Saint Francis said to them: "Make no haste. I shall lay down what you must do for your salvation." From that he conceived the idea of founding the Third Order, of the continents, so called, for the salvation of all men everywhere.

Dismissing them much comforted and disposed to penitence, he withdrew thence to the area between Cannara and Bevagna. He saw some trees beside the road in which was a multitude of different birds as had never before been seen in those parts. Another huge flock was in the open fields beside the trees. Looking at the mass of them wonderingly, with the Spirit of God upon him, Saint Francis said to his companions: "Wait for me here on the road. I shall go and preach to our sisters the birds," and he went into the field where the birds were on the ground. As soon as he began to preach all the birds who were in the trees came down to him, and, like those on the level ground, remained quiet, though he moved among them brushing some with his gown. Not one of them moved at all, relates Brother James of Massa, a holy man who had the story from Brother Masseo who was among the holy father's companions. To these birds Saint Francis said: "My sisters the birds, you have much from God and

43

should always praise him for the free flight you have, for your double and triple plumage, colored and decorated vesture, for your nourishment set out for you without care, for your song accorded you by your Creator, for your number increased for you by the blessing of God, for your race was preserved in the Ark, for the element of the air set apart for you. You neither sow nor reap and God feeds you, gave you rivers and streams at which to drink, mountains, hills, rocks and crags to hide in, tall trees in which to build your nests; and since you cannot spin or weave he gave the garments you need to you and your chicks. It follows that the Creator who so blessed you loves you much. So take care, sisters mine, the birds, not to be ungrateful but be zealous always to praise God."

At these words of the most holy father, all the birds began to open their beaks, stretch their wings and necks and reverently bend their heads to the ground, and with songs and actions to make clear, in manifold ways, that the words pleased them. Saint Francis, when he observed this, was wondrously uplifted in spirit and was amazed at such a host of birds, their most beautiful variety, their mutual love and friendliness. For this he praised the marvellous Creator and gently called them to the Creator's praise.

When he had finished preaching and his exhortation to praise God, he made the sign of the Cross to all the birds, urging them to praise God. Then all the birds took off together, and in the air sang a wonderful great song. This done, following the directions of the sign of the Cross made by the holy father, they parted in order in the four directions, to the east, west, north and south, rising with wondrous song, showing that, as Saint Francis had preached to them, he, the future bearer of the sacred Cross, so, after the shape of the Cross, they divided and with song winged their way to the four quarters of the earth. They showed that the preaching of the Cross, brought to renewal by the most holy father, was to be carried by his brothers through the whole world, for, after the fashion of birds, they called nothing their own on earth, committing themselves wholly to the providence of God.

Chapter 17

The dislike of Saint Francis for the name "master."

FRANCIS, HUMBLE IMITATOR OF CHRIST, aware that the title of master befitted Christ alone, through whom all things were made, used to say that, though he wanted to know and do everything, he did not wish to be called "Master," nor to be known by that name. His reason, of course, was lest he should seem to contravene the Word of God in the Gospel which says that none should be called "master." It was better, he said, in one's poor little state of understanding to be humble, than to do great things and act presumptuously against such majestic written authority, for the name fits only the blessed Christ, all of whose words are perfect. That is why it was laid down by him that no one should presumptuously be called "master" on earth. There is only one true master, the blessed Christ who is God and man, light and life, founder of the world, worthy of praise and glorious for ever and ever. Amen.

Chapter 18

How the death of Saint Francis was revealed to Lady Jacoba of Settesoli.

WHEN THE BLESSED FRANCIS, a few days before his death, was lying ill in the palace of the bishop of Assisi, he would sing some songs of praise along with a few of his companions. And if he for weakness could not join in he would often bid his companions do so. The people of Assisi, fearing lest it should happen that a treasure so peculiarly their own should be held outside Assisi, carefully, with a large armed garrison, guarded the palace day and night. While the holy man was lying ill there, one of his companions said to him: "Father, you know that the men of this earth have great confidence in you and call you a holy man. And so it could be in their minds that, if holiness be in you, as is generally said, you should think of death while you are so gravely ill and rather mourn than sing. The song of praise we sing here is heard by many. This palace on your account is guarded by a host of armed men, so that perhaps they have before them a bad example. That is why I think we should be doing well if we withdrew from here and all went back to Saint Mary of the Angels because it is not good for us to be here among people of the world." The blessed Francis replied to Brother Elias when he said this: "Dearest man, you know that full two years ago, when we were at Foligno, the Lord revealed to me the end of my life and that it will come after a few days of this illness. In the same revelation God gave me assurance of the forgiveness of all my sins and the blessedness of paradise. Up to the day of that revelation I wept about death and my sins, but afterwards I was filled with such joy that I was not able to weep any more but I always remain in joy and gladness. Therefore, I sing, and shall sing, to the Lord who gave me the blessings of grace and made me certain of the blessings of paradise. But I agree about this withdrawal, and do you make ready to carry me there, because I am unable to walk.

So the brothers bore him down in their arms and with a great crowd following set out for Saint Mary of the Angels. When they reached a hospital which is on the way, Saint Francis enquired as to their where-abouts because his vision was dim on account of the blurring of his eyes from his excessive penitence and weeping of past years.

When he learned that they were at the hospital he had himself put on the ground and said: "Turn me towards Assisi." And standing on the road with his face towards the city, he blessed it with many blessings: "Blessed are you in the Lord, because through you many souls will be saved and many servants of the Most High will dwell in you, and through you many will be chosen for the eternal kingdom." These words said, he bade them carry him on.

When they reached Saint Mary's, he called one of his companions and said to him: "Dearest man, God has shown me that on a certain day I shall die, and you know how the Lady Jacoba of Settesoli, a beloved devotee of my heart, will be unconsolably saddened if she is not present at my death. This being so we bid you that she should come now if she would find me living." The brother replied: "You say well, father, for on account of the great devotion she has for you, it would be most improper if she were not at your deathbed." So Saint Francis said: "Bring paper and pen and write as I say to you: 'To the Lady Jacoba, servant

47

of the Most High, Brother Francis, little poor man of Christ, greetings in the Lord and the fellowship of the Holy Spirit. Know, dearest lady, that the blessed Christ has made known to me by his grace that the end of my life draws near. So if you wish to see me living, when you have read this letter, hasten to come to Saint Mary of the Angels, for if you should not come before such and such a day, you will not find me alive. Bring with you a linen cloth in which you will shroud my body and wax for burial. I ask you also to bring some of that food you used to give me when I was sick at Rome.'" While this was actually being written, it was revealed in the Spirit to Saint Francis that the Lady Jacoba was coming to him bringing what he asked. So he said immediately to the scribe: "Write no more. There is no need. Just put the letter aside." The brethren wondered why he did not allow the letter to be finished. And behold, after a few minutes, the Lady Jacoba rang at the door. When the porter answered, he found her with two senior nuns and a large armed escort who had come to Saint Francis. And she had with her everything that he had listed in the letter, for God had revealed to the Lady Jacoba herself while she was praying at Rome that Saint Francis's death was near, and also the needs he had listed in the letter. She carried, too, such a supply of wax that it provided candles not only for the burial but also for masses and sepulchral vigils for many days.

When the abbess came in to Saint Francis, who was still alive, they drew great comfort from seeing each other. Falling at his feet, those which bore the marks of the stigmata, such grace, comfort and flooding tears came on her there that, as Mary Magdalen washed Christ's feet with her tears, so the Lady Jacoba, as though they were the feet of another Christ, devoutly kissing and embracing the feet of Saint Francis, so pressed her faithful lips upon them, that the brethren were not able to pull her away. At length, taken away and questioned how she had come, as if at command, she replied that, when she was praying at night she heard a voice saying: "If you wish to find Brother Francis alive, go without delay to Assisi, and take with you those things which you gave him at Rome when he was ill, and also what is necessary for burial."

The Lady Jacoba remained until the saint departed, and showed great honor to his body. After a space of time, in devotion to Saint Francis, she came to Assisi again. And there, ending her days in holy penitence and virtuous fellowship, she had herself buried in the Church of Saint Francis with great devotion.

Chapter 19

How Christ, the blessed Virgin, Saint John the Baptist, Saint John the Evangelist, together with a host of angels spoke with Saint Francis.

THERE WAS A BOY graced with dovelike purity and angelic innocence, who was received into the Order in the lifetime of the blessed Francis. He was in a small friary where the brothers had no cells, and would sleep on their beds in the open. Saint Francis came to that small friary and in the evening after saying compline he went away to sleep somewhat before the rest, so that he could rise in the night while the rest were asleep. The boy entertained in his heart the wish to seek out carefully where the saint went and what he did when he rose in the night. And so that sleep should not frustrate him, he lay down to rest beside Saint Francis, and tied his cord to that of the saint, so that he would notice when he got up. Saint Francis did not notice this, but he did get up, when all the rest were asleep.

Feeling that his cord was caught, he loosened it from the boy's so carefully that the boy did not perceive it. He went off to a hill near the friary where there was a beautiful wood, to pray alone. But the boy awoke and finding his cord loosed from the saint's, rose immediately, to look for the holy father as he had determined. When he found the gate open which led to the wood, observing that the saint had gone there, the boy went into the wood and proceeded to the top of the hill which has been mentioned. There Saint Francis had paused to pray. When the boy had stopped a short distance away he heard many voices speaking. Approaching closer the more clearly to hear what was being said, he saw a wondrous light all round Saint Francis, and in that light he saw Christ, the Virgin Mary, the blessed John the Baptist and John the Evangelist, and a great host of angels speaking with the blessed Francis. Seeing all this the boy fell into an ecstasy, and trembling at what he had heard, fell as if dead on to the path by which the saint would return to the friary.

When the wondrous conversation was over Saint Francis was returning, and since it was still deep night he stumbled over the body of the boy lying as if dead on the path. Pitying him and lifting him in his holy arms as a good shepherd does his own little lamb, the saint carried him back to bed. Learning later the vision he had seen, he bade the boy to tell no one in his lifetime. He kept the secret, grew up in great favor with God and devotion to Saint Francis, and finished his life a great man in the Order. After Saint Francis died he revealed the whole of this story. To the praise of our Lord Jesus Christ.

Chapter 20

Concerning the resolution adopted at the general chapter at Saint Mary of the Angels and Saint Dominic who was also present.

AT A CHAPTER-GENERAL which God's most faithful servant Saint Francis held at Saint Mary of the Angels, were gathered 5,000 brethren, and Saint Dominic, together with seven of his brethren, was present. Also present was Lord Cardinal Ugolino, a devotee of Saint Francis and his Order. And since the papal court was at the time at Perugia, the cardinal was careful to come to Assisi and used to come to see Saint Francis every day, and whenever he sang mass he would preach a sermon to the brethren.

When he came to visit that holy gathering and saw the participants in companies of sixties, hundreds, and three hundreds sitting in the plain in godly conversation, prayer and tears, or in manifestations of affection, and amid such silence that there was no din or noise there, in wonder he would say of such a multitude: "The ordered battleline of God," and it moved him to tears of devotion. No one among them dared to tell stories or jests but wherever they were gathered together they prayed, lamented, or spoke of the soul's salvation. They lived on the plain in groups with separate buildings made of latticed sticks for walls and roof. That is why this assembly was called the chapter of wicker and mats. They slept on the bare ground or a little straw, with pillows of stone or wood. Such was the universal devotion that from the nearby papal court came counts and barons, in large numbers, knights and squires, cardinals in person with bishops and priests, and there gathered round them nobles and common folk to see such a holy gathering of saintly humble men the like of which the world had never yet witnessed, and also to see their worshipful head Saint Francis, who had snatched such a holy and beautiful treasure from the hands of the world and turned a flock so devoted into the fold of Christ.

When they were all gathered together, the holy pastor and venerable leader Francis rose, in the power of the Holy Spirit, and expounded the word of life to the blessed flock with a voice as loud as a trumpet which God's anointing conferred on him. This is the theme he set before them: "We have promised great things but greater things are promised us. Let us keep the former and aspire to the latter. Pleasure is brief, punishment everlasting. Suffering is brief. Glory has no end." In addition to these words, devoutly preaching, he called them all to obedience to Holy Mother Church and to the sweetness of brotherly love, to prayer for all the holy people of God, to patience in adversity, to clean living and angelic purity, to peace and concord with God and men, to humility and gentleness before all, to contempt for the world, and burning zeal for evangelical poverty, to care and watchfulness in heavenly prayer and God's praise, to casting aside all care and anxiety of soul and body on to the good pastor of our souls and bodies, our Lord, the blessed Jesus Christ. "And that is why I bid you, brothers here assembled, in the name of your saving obedience, that no one of you have any concern or anxiety about food or any other bodily necessity, but that you should give your whole attention to prayer and praise to God, casting all your care on Christ, because he has a special care for us." And so they all did, hastening to prayer with cheerful mind.

But Saint Dominic, who was present on this occasion, marvelling at Saint Francis's command, and judging him to have acted unwisely in such an enormous gathering, in commanding that no one should take thought for the necessary concerns of the body, was of the opinion that a lamentable situation would arise. But the Lord Jesus Christ, wishing to show that he had a special care for his beloved sheep and his own poor ones, made obvious the hand of the Lord on the folk of Assisi, Spoleto and all adjacent communities. They came with donkeys, mules and horses all loaded with bread and wine, beans and cheese and all the things they thought those blessed poor had need of, and could use. And they brought besides tablecloths, vessels large and small, and whatever utensils were necessary. And he who could serve them most devotedly and attentively, considered himself the more blessed in zealous provision for their needs. And you might have seen there knights and nobles gladly and devoutly serving the gathering of the saints. You might have seen devoted members of the clergy running round everywhere like common servants, and fine young men serving with so much reverence that they seemed to be serving not poor little friars, but the apostles of our Lord Jesus Christ.

When Saint Dominic saw all this, and truly observed there the providence of God, humbly rebuking himself for his judgment on his earlier indiscretion, he knelt before Saint Francis and humbly confessed his fault thus: "Truly God has care for these little poor folk and I know it not. So from now I promise to observe holy evangelical poverty, and I curse in God's name all brethren of my Order who have presumed as members to have personal possessions."

Saint Dominic was truly edified by the faith of Saint Francis, by the obedience and poverty of so great and holy a colleague, divine providence and most abundant provision of all things. Like the holy and wise man that he was, he recognized the utter faithfulness of God in all his words, for just as he makes the vines and the lilies grow and feeds the birds of the air, so he provides all that is needful for his holy poor.

At that chapter it was made known to Saint Francis that many were wearing iron breastplates and iron rings against their flesh, which made some ill, hindered the prayers of many and caused the death of some. So, like a most gentle and true father, he told them to put off such things before him in the name of their obedience. And there were found a good five hundred breastplates, and iron rings for the arms and trunk in such abundance, that made one huge heap which he ordered to be left there.

Afterwards the holy father taught and comforted them all and told them how to escape this present world with God's blessing and his, and with spiritual joy sent them all back comforted to their own provinces. To the praise and glory of God.

Chapter 21

How God spoke to Saint Francis and how Saint Francis caused wine to grow on a vine without grapes.

WHEN SAINT FRANCIS had a grave eye affliction the Lord Cardinal Ugolino, the protector of Saint Francis who loved him deeply, bade him to go to Rieti where there were the best ophthalmologists. The blessed Francis, when he received the Lord Cardinal's letter, went first to Saint Damian's where Saint Clare lived. His purpose was to visit and console her before his retreat, going to Rieti later.

When he reached Saint Damian's he was so severely

hampered by his eye-trouble that he could not distinguish any light at all. So Saint Clare had a little cell of reeds and rushes built so that he might rest in greater confidence further away. He stayed there fifty days, but was so plagued by his eye-trouble, and by a swarm of mice stirred up by the Devil that he was unable to rest night or day. The most blessed Francis, recognizing that this was a scourge from God, began to give God thanks and to praise him with his whole heart and voice, and to cry out from his deepest being that he was worthy of such tricks and troubles and much greater ones than these. And he prayed to the Lord saying: "Lord Jesus Christ, good shepherd, grant me, your little sheep, grace and virtue that in no trouble, tribulation or grief I may depart from you."

Thereupon, a voice came from heaven saying: "Francis, reply to me: if the whole world were gold and the sea, rivers and springs were balm, and all the mountains and stones and springs were gems, and you could find a treasure as much nobler than them all by as much as gold is more precious than them all, and balm more precious than water, and gems than mountains and rocks, and if all that precious treasure were granted you for your present infirmity, should you not rejoice?" Saint Francis answered: "Lord, I am not worthy of such treasure." And the Lord said to him: "Rejoice now, Brother Francis, for such is the treasure of eternal life which I have set aside for you, and from now I clothe you with that infirmity, and your affliction is the earnest of that blessed treasure."

Then Saint Francis, thrilled with gladness, called his companion and said: "Let us go to Rieti to the Lord Cardinal." And consoling the blessed Clare with godly words which flowed with honey, and wishing her humbly goodbye as he usually did, he took the road to Rieti.

When he drew near that place, such a host of people poured out to meet him that he would not go into the city but turned aside to a church some two miles away.

But the people, knowing that he was staying there, flocked to meet him in such crowds, that the vineyard of the priest of that church (it was time to harvest the grapes) was completely despoiled and the fruit eaten. The priest was so upset at the sight of such damage that he was sorry he had allowed Saint Francis into his church. Saint Francis, learning this from the Holy Spirit, had the priest summoned, and said: "Dearest Father, how many measures of wine does this vineyard produce for you in a good season?" "Twelve," was the reply. Said Saint Francis: "Therefore, I beg you, Father, to bear with my remaining in this your church because of the peace I find here. And allow everyone to receive of your grapes for the love of God and of me, his little poor one, and I promise you in the name of my Lord Jesus Christ that this year you shall gather twenty measures." This Saint Francis did because of the great harvest of souls that God was gathering there. He saw many of the visitors drunk with the love of God, and, forgetting the world, converted to longings for heaven. So he saw the despoiling of the material vineyard a more useful outcome than making the vineyard of the Lord of Hosts barren of heavenly wine.

Trusting therefore the promises of the saint, the priest generously abandoned his vineyard to feed the visitors. Wondrously then was the vineyard stripped bare and eaten up by them, so that scarcely a few little bunches remained. Vintage time came, and the priest, trusting in the saint's promise, gathered together those few poor bunches of grapes and, placing them in their accustomed press, as the saint had promised, he obtained twenty measures of the best wine that year. Thus it was demonstrated that, just as through the merits of Saint Francis the ruined vineyard had produced wine more abundantly, so Christian people, sterile in sin, through his teachings may move abundantly into the fruits of penitence. To the glory of our Lord Jesus Christ.

Chapter 22

How Saint Francis appeared in glory with many holy friars to a certain friar in a state of ecstasy.

A CERTAIN NOBLE and gently nurtured young man came to the Order of Saint Francis. He was clothed in the friars' habit, but, after a few days, at the Devil's prompting, he developed such a dislike for the habit he wore that it seemed to him he wore the most loathsome sackcloth. He abhorred the sleeves, he hated the hood; the length and the coarseness of the robe seemed to him a burden too hard to bear. So it came about that with growing disgust of the Order he took it in mind to cast off the habit and return to secular life. Now his master had taught him that whenever he passed in front of the altar of the friary in which was kept the most holy body of Christ, with great reverence, bended knees, uncovered head and crossed arms, he should devoutly bow. This he was always careful to do.

It happened that on the night he had thought to abandon the habit and return to secular life, he had to pass the altar, and as his custom was he bent his knees. He immediately fell into a rapture and a wondrous vision was shown to him. A limitless host seemed to pass in procession before him. They were the redeemed and moved two by two, clad in the most gorgeous and precious robes. Their faces, hands, and any part of their person which could be seen, shone more brightly than the sun. They processed with song and canticle of angels most solemnly and chanting sweetly. Among them went two more nobly clothed than the rest with such brightness that they struck speechless amazement into those who beheld them. Almost at the end of the procession, he saw someone endowed with such glory as befitted a new knight outstandingly honored.

The youth wondered much when he saw this but did not know what it meant. He did not dare to ask those who passed by, nor was he able to do so, overwhelmed as he was with such sweetness. But when the procession had passed and the last of them was still in sight, he took courage and rushed up to them and asked: "Dearest friends, I beg you, please, who are the wondrous beings who make up this procession?" Turning their most shining faces to him they made reply: "We are all friars minor who have but now come from paradise." Further questioning he said: "Who are those two who shine so brightly among the rest?" They replied: "Those two who are brighter than the rest are Saint Francis and Saint Antony. That last one, so excellently honored is a holy brother lately dead whom we are escorting to the joys of the everlasting kingdom, with glory and triumph along with both saints and holy angels, because be battled strongly against temptations and persisted in his holy calling. These robes of silk, which we so gloriously wear, were given us in place of the coarse habits which we endured patiently in the Order, and the brightness of glory which you see was given us by God because of the humble penitence we made, and for the holy poverty, obedience and purest chastity which we preserved with joyous heart right to the end. So, son, let it not seem hard to you to wear the fruitful sackcloth of the Order; for if you keep yourself in the sackcloth of the blessed Francis, for the love of our Lord Jesus Christ, scorning the world, mortifying the flesh, and battling like a true man against the Devil, you will shine in like garments along with us."

At these words, the young man came to himself and consoled by that vision cast all his temptation aside.

He confessed his fault before the warden and the rest of the brethren. Henceforth he took pleasure as if they were riches, in the harshness of penitence and coarseness of garment. So, changed for the better he ended in a life of sanctity. To the praise of our Lord Jesus Christ. Amen.

Chapter 23

How a ravening wolf was tamed by Saint Francis.

A REMARKABLE THING TOOK PLACE, worth wide remembrance, in the community of Gubbio. While Saint Francis was still alive, in the region thereabouts was a fearful wolf, enormous in size and most ferocious in the savagery of his hunger. It had devoured not only animals but men and women too, so much that it held all the people in such terror that they all went armed whenever they went into the country-side as if they were off to grim war. Even armed, they were not able to escape the tearing teeth and ravening rage of the wolf, if by mischance they met him. Such terror gripped them all that scarcely anyone dared to go outside the city gate.

It was God's will to emphasize for those townsfolk the holiness of Saint Francis, since the blessed father was at that very time among them. In pity for them he made arrangements to go out and meet the wolf. "Have care, Brother Francis, not to go outside the gate," they said, "because the wolf who has devoured many will surely kill you." But Saint Francis, hoping in the Lord Jesus Christ who rules the spirits of all flesh, without the protection of shield or helmet, but guarding himself with the Sign of the Holy Cross, went out of the gate with a companion, putting all his trust in the Lord who makes all who believe in him "walk without harm over viper and asp, but tread not only on the wolf, but on the lion too and the serpent." So the most faithful Francis went fearlessly out to meet the wolf. Many were watching from places they had climbed to see. That fearsome wolf rushed out against Saint Francis and his friend with open mouth. The blessed father met him with the Sign of the Cross, and by divine strength restrained the wolf from himself and his companion, checked its charge and closed his cruelly open mouth. Calling him then, he said: "Come to me, brother wolf, and in Christ's name I command you not to harm me or anybody." It is wondrous that one Sign of the Cross closed that awful maw. As soon as the order was given, like a lamb and not a wolf, with lowered head he laid himself at the feet of the saint. Saint Francis said to him: "Brother wolf, you wreak much harm in these parts and have done some dreadful deeds, destroying creatures of God without mercy. Not only brute beasts do you kill but, a deed of more hateful boldness, you kill and devour men and women made in the image of God. So you deserve an awful death, to be hacked like any footpad or loathly murderer. That is why all justly cry out and murmur against you and the whole city is your foe. But, brother wolf, I want you and them to make peace so that they may be no more harmed by you, nor the hounds further pursue you."

The wolf showed by movements of his body, tail and ears and the bowing of its head, that he accepted without reservation what the saint said. Saint Francis continued: "Brother wolf, in view of your undertaking to make this peace, I promise you that as long as you live you will be given what you need by the people of this community, so that you will no more suffer hunger, for I know that whatever evil you do you do because of the ravening of hunger. But, my brother wolf, since I secure such favor for you, I want you to promise me that you will never harm any animal or man. Do you so promise?" And the wolf by proper bowing of his head showed that he promised to keep the undertakings put to him by the saint. Saint Francis said: "Brother wolf, I want you to give me a pledge that I can confidently accept that you will keep your promise," and when Saint Francis held out his hand to receive the pledge, the wolf lifted his right front paw and softly and gently placed it in Saint Francis' hand, giving such pledge as he could. Then said Saint Francis: "Brother wolf, I bid you in the name of the Lord Jesus Christ to come along with me, without fear, into the city to make this peace in the name of Jesus Christ." The wolf immediately set off to go with the saint like the gentlest lamb.

Seeing this, the citizens were dumbfounded. The miracle echoed through the community so that men and women, great and small, congregated in the square where Saint Francis was with the wolf. The populace was there in a horde when Saint Francis rose and preached a wondrous sermon. It was, he said, because of their sins that such scourges were allowed; and how much more perilous was the flame of Gehenna's fire which can devour the damned for ever, than the ravening of a wolf which can kill only the body; and how terrible it was to be plunged into the jaws of hell when one poor animal could hold so huge a crowd in panic and peril. "Return, therefore, dear friends, to the Lord and do proper penance, and God will free you from the wolf now, and in the future from the pit of consuming fire. Listen, dear folk, for brother wolf who is present here has promised me and pledged his word to make peace with you, to do no one harm if you promise to give him his daily necessities. And on his behalf I promise and pledge to you that he will faithfully observe the pact of peace." Then all there gathered with a mighty shout promised to feed the wolf for ever. And Saint Francis said to the wolf before them all: "And do you, brother wolf, promise to keep faith with them, and do harm to neither man nor beast." The wolf knelt and bowed his head, and with conciliatory movements of body, tail and ears, indicated that he would keep his promise.

Saint Francis said: "Brother wolf, just as you gave me your word outside the gate, here now before these people give me your word that you will not betray me." Then the wolf lifted his right paw and pledged himself with everyone standing round. All were lost in joy and wonder as much for the devotion of the saint as for the strangeness of the miracle, and they made the welkin ring acclaiming the peace of wolf and people, praising and blessing the Lord Jesus Christ who sent Saint Francis to them. By his merits he freed them from the fear of the loathly beast, and out of so awful a visitation, restored to them peace and quiet.

Both kept the pact Saint Francis had arranged, and for two years the wolf went from door to door begging. Harming no one, and harmed by no one, he lived like a state ward. It was wonderful that no dog barked at him. At length he grew old and died, and the citizens mourned him, for by his peaceful and kind forbearance, he recalled to mind the worth and holiness of Saint Francis whenever he went through the town. To the praise and glory of the Lord Jesus Christ. Amen.

Chapter 24

How Saint Francis liberated turtle doves and made nests for them.

A LAD FROM SIENNA snared in a birdtrap a big flock of doves and was carrying them all off alive to sell. But Saint Francis, who was always full of love and especially towards domestic animals and wondrous compassionate towards birds, seeing these doves, and moved with love and pity, said to the boy who was carrying them: "Good lad, I beg you, do hand over those doves to me, so that such innocent birds, which in the Bible are the symbols of pure, humble and faithful souls, may not fall into the hands of cruel people who will kill them." Inspired by God, the boy immediately handed them all over to Saint Francis. The holy father took them into his arms and began speaking to them. Sweetly he began to speak to them: "My sister doves, pure and innocent, why did you let yourselves be trapped? I want to rescue you from death, and make you nests, so that you may be fruitful and fulfil your Creator's commandment to multiply." Off went Francis and made a dovecote for them all.

The doves, taking up their nests built by Saint Francis, laid eggs and grew in number among the friars, and showed such friendship to the saint and the brothers, that they seemed like the hens which the brothers kept. They never went out without Saint Francis's blessing and permission. He said to the lad who gave him the doves: "Son, someday you will be a friar minor in this Order, and gracefully serve the Lord Jesus Christ." And so it fell out. He entered the

Order and lived a commendable and exemplary life to the end, thanks to the merits of the holy father. To the praise of our Lord Jesus Christ. Amen.

Chapter 25

The miraculous statue that appeared to Saint Francis on which he prophesied the fifteen-fold status of the Order.

ONCE WHEN SAINT FRANCIS was devoutly praying to the Most High in a chapel of Saint Mary of the Angels, there came before his mortal eyes a right marvellous vision, a mighty statue just as Nebuchadnezzar saw in his dream. It had a head of gold and a most beautiful face, arms and breast of silver, loins and legs of brass, shins of iron, feet part iron and part earthenware, and it was dressed in sackcloth of which it seemed ashamed. The blessed Francis, gazing on the statue, was truly astonished at its almost indescribable beauty, its wondrous size, and its apparent shame of the sackcloth in which it was clad. As he thus mused and gazed, the statue itself seemed to say: "Why such amazement? God sent you in me this example to teach you the future of your Order. The head and handsome face is the beginning of your Order, founded in wide evangelical perfection. Just as the substance of gold itself is more precious than other metals, and the position of the head is up above the other members, so the beginning of your Order will be of such great worth in brotherly love; of such great beauty because of angelic honor, and such height because of the

64

evangelical poverty at which all the world shall wonder. The Queen of Sheba, that is the Holy Church, will wonder in her heart, when she sees in the first chosen brethren of your Order, such beauty of holiness and glow of spiritual wisdom as if it shone back in angelic mirrors. Blessed will they be who have been zealous to reflect, in total conformity to Christ, the virtues and the ways of those precious stones around the heads of gold, clinging more to their heavenly beauty than to the deceits of the flowering world.

"The chest and arms of silver will be the second condition of your Order, which will stand below the first, just as silver is less valuable than gold. And just as silver has worth, clarity and fine sound, so in that second state there will be many precious brethren renowned in holy writ, in the clear light of holiness and the echo of the Word of God, uplifted to the place where many of them will become popes, cardinals and bishops. And because a man's strength is manifested in chest and arms, so, at that period, God will raise up in your Order men like silver in their knowledge, and famed for goodness who, as much by their learning as by their goodness, will defend religion and even the Church Universal from the various assaults of devils, and the manifold attacks of wicked men. But though that generation will be wonderful, it will still not attain the utter perfection of the first, but so will stand in its reputation as silver stands beside gold.

"After this will be a third condition in your Order which will be represented by bronze loins, and thighs, but, just as bronze is valued less than silver, so those of the third estate will be valued less than those of the second; and just as like bronze in numbers and in geographical spread they will excel, yet in matters of religion they will be confined to those whose knowledge is of earthly things. And though, because of their knowledge, they will have speech, sonorous

65

and wondrous like the speech of bronze, and because
they will be things of the loins and legs, alas! they will
be counted by God, as the apostle puts it, "sounding
brass and jangling cymbals," because they echo back
the words of others, and as if from the thighs, get
themselves spiritual sons, and though showing to
others the spring of life, are themselves dead in
drought, and themselves thanks to their arid loins will
cling to the earth. May God's mercy aid you. Amen.
After them will come the terrible and terrifying fourth
estate revealed to you in the iron shins, for as iron
tames and scatters bronze, silver and gold, so that
estate will be of such iron depravity, that from its icy
chill, awful rust and the iron ways of that perilous
period, it will bring to oblivion the good and golden
love of the pioneers, the silvern trunk of those who
followed them, and the bronze, if noisy, talkativeness
of the third group which it had built into the Church
of Christ. However, just as the shins hold up the body,
so those with a certain sturdiness of iron hypocrisy will
keep upright the body of the Order; and just as the
loins, so the shins will lie hidden beneath the vest-
ments and the habits of religion, so they, serving the
loins, and lying hidden from the world, rusty as iron,
but obvious to God, have brought much to nought
under the hammer of their evil living. Therefore will
they be afflicted like the hardest iron with the first of
tribulation and the hammers of shocking trials. It is
thus that they will be burned with the demonic
disasters of the rulers of the world, and the fires and
coals of the age, that they may learn to suffer
tribulation. And because they have sinned by irrev-
erence and hardness, they will be most grievously
tormented by the irreverent. Because of those trials,
they will be stirred to such a high degree of
impatience, for, just as iron resists all metals, so they
will set themselves against everybody, obstinately
resisting not only secular but even spiritual author-
ities, thinking that, like iron, they can trample

66

everyone down, whereby they will greatly displease God.

"The fifth condition will be part iron in as much as hypocrisy is involved, and part earthy, in as much as they will be totally bound up with the cares of this world. And just as you saw from the feet that pottery based on baked clay and iron appeared mingled, but which could in no way be unified, so it will be in that last state of the Order, because there will arise such a loathly division between grasping hypocrites and earthly creatures, baked together from the mire of worldly things and the lust of the flesh; because thanks to their deep discord, like earthenware and iron, they will be unable to have fellowship together. And they will hold in scorn not only the Gospel and the Rule, but equally will trample with their iron and earthy feet, that is, by their unclean and base affections, every rule of discipline of their holy Order. And just as earthenware and iron are divided from each other, so shall their external and internal divisions be. Living contentiously within themselves, their external relations shall be to party and worldly dictatorships. So they will come into such universal disapproval that not only will they find it hard to live and to dwell in countries, they will hardly be able to wear the habit openly. Many of them will be punished and destroyed by men of this world with shocking torments, because every house and place of habitation will shun such polluted feet. All of this will fall upon them because they have withdrawn from the golden head. Blessed will be they who, in those days of danger will return to the injunctions of the precious head, because the Lord has tried them like gold in a furnace, and shall crown them like a rich sacrifice, and receive them for ever.

"This habit, of which I seem ashamed, is holy poverty. Of the whole Order it is the grace, and glory, the only custodian, the crown and foundation of every kind of sanctity. Yet, when virtuous zeal fails, degenerate apostates will become ashamed of holy poverty, and casting off their cheap garments, will choose expensive ones, and will wear in their hypocritical boldness empty headgear. Happy, indeed, and blessed they who shall continue to the end in those things they have promised to the Lord."

These words said, the statue disappeared. Saint Francis, in deep wonder, like a good shepherd, commended to God Omnipotent the sheep he had, and those which were yet to be, with many tears. Praise and glory for ever to our Lord Jesus Christ.

Chapter 26

The vision of Saint Francis in which demons were unable to enter the friary of Saint Mary of the Angels.

ON ONE OCCASION when Saint Francis was at the friary of the Porziuncula, giving himself devoutly to prayer as his custom was, he saw the whole place beset and besieged, as with an army, by demons. But none of them was able to get into the place because, since the brothers were of such great sanctity, they had no one to get in by. But one of the brothers, stirred to anger and impatience against a colleague, made up vindictive accusations against him. The gate of virtue thrown down, and the door of wickedness opened, a way of entry was available to a demon. Immediately before Saint Francis's eyes, one of those demons entered the friary and attacked that brother, as an aggressor attacks a bound foe. But the holy father and pastor, who was watching most faithfully over the care of his flock, seeing that the wolf had gone in to devour one of his little ewes, and aware in his heart that the lamb had been placed in great danger, quickly had the brother in question called to him. When he had obediently hurried to so anxious a shepherd, Saint Francis told him to reveal the poison he had mixed against his brother and kept in his heart, and which had betrayed him into the enemy's hands. Terrified, he bared his wound, confessed his sin, and humbly sought pardon with penance. This done, absolved from his fault, and with penance accepted, he was immediately abandoned by the demon, in Saint Francis's full view. A sheep snatched from the maw of a savage beast, he returned thanks to God and Saint Francis and by his shepherd's merits continued to the end in holy living. To the praise of the Lord Jesus Christ and of the Holy Father. Amen.

Chapter 27

How Saint Francis converted the Sultan of Babylon to the faith.

OUR MOST HOLY FATHER FRANCIS, spurred by zeal for God and longing for martyrdom, with twelve most holy brethren, crossed the sea, proposing to go straight to the Sultan. When they reached a country of infidels in which such cruel people guarded the roads that no Christian could traverse them alive, they none the less, by God's grace, evaded death. However, captured and tortured in many ways and tightly bound, they were taken to the Sultan. Before him, Saint Francis, by the prompting of the Holy Spirit, preached so divinely about the Catholic faith, that he offered to prove it by fire. That is why the Sultan gained so high an opinion of him, as much for his firmness of faith as for his contempt of the world. Though he was utterly poor he would accept nothing and he longed for martyrdom. He gladly listened to him and frequently sought his company. Further, he generously made it possible for Francis and his associates to go wherever they desired and preach anywhere in his whole Empire, and he gave them a certain talisman the sight of which saved them from harm by anyone.

So this generous concession granted, Saint Francis sent out his associates two by two into all parts of the pagan world. But Saint Francis, seeing that he was not able to gather there the harvest he longed for, decided to reassemble his brethren and, at God's direction, to return to Christendom. He reported this to the Sultan, who replied: "Brother Francis, I would gladly be converted to the faith of Christ but I am afraid to do so because these Saracens would forthwith assassinate me and you and your companions if they knew. But since you still have much to do, and I have much important business also to do for the salvation of my soul, I would not gladly wish to bring untimely death to either of us. But show me how I may be saved, and I am prepared to obey you in all particulars." Saint Francis said to him: "Sire, I shall indeed return home, but after I go to heaven, at God's call, after my death, as God wills, I will send you two of my brethren, from whom you will receive baptism and be saved, as my Lord Jesus Christ has revealed to me. Do you meanwhile emancipate yourself from all which binds you, that when the grace of Christ shall come, it may find you prepared in faith and devotion." The Sultan gladly agreed and faithfully obeyed. Saint Francis bade him farewell and returned to Christendom.

After a few years, the Sultan fell ill. And in expectation of the saint's promise (he had already passed to the better life), he set watchers at all the gates with orders that, if two friars in the garb of Saint Francis should appear, they were to be brought to him in all haste. It was at that very time that Saint Francis appeared to two of his brethren, and told them to proceed without delay to the Sultan, and bring him the promised salvation. Religiously they carried out the order. They crossed the sea to the Sultan and were brought to him by the watchers mentioned. When he saw them he rejoiced with exceeding joy saying: "Now I know truly that God has sent me his servants at God's direction to pass on to me my salvation." Receiving from those brethren the tokens of faith and holy baptism he was born again in his sickness, and in the Lord passed to eternal bliss, his soul saved by the merits of Saint Francis. To the glory of Christ. Amen.

Chapter 28

How Saint Francis cured a certain leper of leprosy of the soul while he was still alive.

WHILE STILL LIVING in this wretched and lamentable world, the blessed Francis, enlightened by the Holy Spirit, with all his strength, always did his utmost to tread in the footprints of our Lord Jesus Christ. So it was that, just as Christ condescended to become a pilgrim, so the blessed Francis manifested himself and his Order as pilgrims, and even had it written into his Rule, that all his brethren should serve the Lord as pilgrims and strangers in this world. Further, just as Christ came to heal lepers, healing and cleansing them in body, but was also prepared to die for them, making them whole and clean in soul, so too, the blessed Francis, desiring to be utterly conformed to Christ, served lepers with the utmost love, providing them with food, washing their rotting limbs, cleansing their garments, and hastening warmly to kiss them. He directed, too, that the brethren of his Order, for the love of Christ who was willing to be reputed a leper for our sakes, should everywhere attentively serve them. Like true children of obedience this the brethren most readily did.

At a certain friary where the brothers had a lazar-house, one leper was such an evil fellow, impatient and violent, that no one had a doubt that he was tormented by an evil spirit. He belabored the brothers who served him with horrible curses and physical injuries, and wounded them with lashings and pummellings. Further, and this is truly the worst of all, he kept on blaspheming the blessed Christ and his most holy Mother and other saints. So although in the midst of the injuries and blows inflicted on them the brothers did their best to store up the merit of long-suffering, their conscience was unable to endure the blasphemies against Christ and his most holy Mother. Nor did they want to appear accessories to the crime. So they decided to abandon the man, lest they should be tools of the Devil and a blasphemer of God. But they did not want to do this until they had told the whole story in order to Saint Francis who at the time was staying at another friary. When he heard the story, Saint Francis came to the leper and said: "God give you peace, dearest brother." "What sort of peace is there for me?" he replied. "No, God has taken my peace and I am rotten from head to foot." Saint Francis said: "Dearest man, be patient, because the infirmities which here are carried into your body will emerge to the salvation of your soul, if they be borne placidly." He replied: "How can I bear it placidly when my torture goes on day and night? Not only am I burned up and tortured by my illness, but I am afflicted harshly by your brothers who are appointed to look after me. No one does what he should for me."

But Saint Francis, recognizing by the Holy Spirit

that the man was troubled by an evil spirit, went and made devout prayer to God. Then he came back and said: "Dearest man, I myself am willing to serve you, since the rest do not satisfy you." The man replied: "I am glad, but what can you do more than the others?" Saint Francis said: "I will do whatever you wish." And he: "I want you to give me a bath. I stink in such a fashion I cannot endure myself."

Saint Francis had water heated with many fragrant herbs in it. He undressed the leper with his own holy hands and began to wash him, and another brother poured water over him. And as the water washed him on the outside, so he was totally cleansed of the leprosy, and inside his spirit was cleansed and healed. And just as his body was washed and cleansed of leprosy, so his soul was baptized in tears and cleansed from sin. So, when he saw he was being healed bodily, with the same completeness he was anointed and healed in spirit. He burst into such penitence and tears, that he cried out aloud: "I am worthy of hell for the harm I have done your brothers, for the blows and lashes I have put on them, and for my impatience and blasphemy against God." For fifteen days he kept bitterly lamenting his sins with extraordinary wailing which burst from his inner being. He sought nothing but the mercy of God and with that conviction and with weeping he confessed all his sins to a priest.

The blessed Francis seeing so notable a miracle and thanking God went away to a far country, before the news spread and everyone came running to him, a situation which in his humility he utterly rejected. Like a wise and faithful servant of God he took the utmost care to render glory and honor to God and take only shame and ignominy for himself.

The leper, a little while after his wondrous cleansing and repentance fell ill and well armed with the sacraments of the Church, departed this life. Saint Francis was praying in a wood near a distant friary when the dead leper appeared to him, more resplendent than the sun, and said: "Do you recognize me? I am the leper whom on your promise the blessed Christ cleansed. Today I go to paradise and the realm of the blessed, for which I thank almighty God and you. Blessed be your soul and body, and blessed be your words and works, because through you many souls are being saved and shall be saved hereafter. And know that there is not a day on which the holy angels and all the saints do not render great thanks to God for the holy fruits now reaped by you and your Order through the world. Be comforted, thank God and be blessed of God." At this he disappeared and Saint Francis remained deeply comforted.

Chapter 29

The three robbers converted by Saint Francis, to one of whom were revealed the tortures of hell and the glory of paradise.

THE MOST BLESSED FATHER FRANCIS, eager to lead all men to Christ, went through many parts of the world. Wherever he went, since he was led by the Holy Spirit, he won a new family for God. Like a vessel chosen of God for the dispensing of the balm of grace, he went to Slavonia, the march of Trivigina, the march of Anconia, Apulia, to the land of the Saracens, and to many other provinces, everywhere increasing the servants of our Lord Jesus Christ.

So it came about that, when he was journeying through the fortress of Monte Casale, he met a young nobleman of San Sepolcro, who said: "Father, I would gladly become one of your brothers." Saint Francis replied: "Son, you are a young nobleman, gently nurtured. Perhaps you would not be able to endure our poverty?" But he replied: "Father, are you not men as I am? Just as you, who are men like me, can endure it, so too shall I, God helping me." This reply pleased Saint Francis greatly. He received him forthwith and blessed him, giving him the name of Brother Angelo. He conducted himself with such grace that a little later he made him warden of Monte Casale.

At that time, there were three notable bandits in that part of the country who were guilty of many evil deeds. One day they came to the friary and asked Brother Angelo to give them food. Refusing them with stern reproaches, he said: "You thieves and savage murderers are not only unashamed to prey on the toils of others, but, furthermore, impudent as you are, presume to feed on the alms given to God's servants. You are unworthy of a place on earth. You have no respect for men, and hold God who made you in contempt. So get about your business and never come back here again." Upset at this, they went off in great wrath. But, behold, Saint Francis came back that same day, bringing from his and his companion's begging, a wallet of bread and a bottle of wine.

When the warden told how he had rebuffed the bandits, Saint Francis severely rebuked him, saying he had acted wickedly, because sinners are best won back by the sweetness of piety than by harsh anger. "Our Lord Christ whose Gospel we have promised to serve said: 'The healthy do not need a physician, but those who are sick' and 'I came not to call the righteous but sinners to repentance.' He often ate with sinners. Thus you have acted uncharitably and against the example of Jesus Christ. I bid you therefore in holy obedience to take this wallet of bread, and flask of wine, which I have begged. Seek out those robbers diligently over hill and valley till you find them. You will give to them all this bread and wine in my name, and then you will kneel before them and humbly confess your sin of inconsiderateness and cruelty. And beg them in my name not to go on with their evil deeds but fear God and not harm their neighbors. If they do this I promise to go on providing for their bodily needs. When you have done this humble service return." Meanwhile Saint Francis prayed to the Lord that he might soften their hearts to repentance.

So it came about that when the robbers had eaten the alms sent by Saint Francis they began in their turn to confer. "Alas, wretched and miserable men whom the hard punishment of hell awaits. We go about not only robbing and wounding but even killing men. And yet we are affected by no fear of God or prick of conscience for such awful crimes and murders. Yet behold, this holy friar has just come to us, and on account of some very true words he justly said to us about our wickedness, here before us has humbly accused himself. And moreover he has brought the generous promise of the holy father and the love-gift of bread and wine. Truly these are the saints of God who deserve the heavenly fatherland. We are the sons of eternal perdition, who daily shall the more justify the avenging flames for our unutterable crimes. I do not know whether we can find mercy from God for the crimes we have committed or the evil deeds we have done." At these words the other two said: "What then must we do?" The first said: "Let us go to Saint Francis, and if he can offer us confidence that we can find mercy from God for our sins, let us do whatever he commands to free our souls from the pit of hell."

They all heartily agreed and hurried to Saint Francis saying: "Father, because of our many heinous sins we are sure that we cannot find mercy from God. But if you believe that God can receive us into his mercy, see, we are ready to do penance and obey you in all that you bid." Saint Francis received them with kindness and love, and encouraging them by many examples, made them confident of receiving the mercy of God. And he further promised he would obtain for them from the Lord that mercy and grace, teaching them that the boundless mercy of God's grace surpasses all our sins though they be beyond measure, and how, as the Gospel and the Apostle Paul had it, Jesus Christ came into this world to save sinners.

Through such wholesome instructions those three robbers renounced the world, and received by the holy father, they followed him in garb and spirit. Two of them lived only a short time after so praiseworthy a transformation. They passed at God's call from this world. The third lived on, his great sins always in mind, and subjected himself to such penance that for fifteen continuous years, except for the lenten fasts which he kept like the rest, three days a week he lived on bread and water only. Content with only one garment, he always went round barefoot and never slept after matins. After those fifteen years, Saint Francis went from this world to the Heavenly Father.

The one-time robber kept up this strict regime of penitence for many years. One night after matins, so strong a desire for sleep fell on him that by no means could he resist it, and keep awake as he commonly did. When he could not longer resist nor had the strength to pray, falling to the temptation, he lay upon his bed and slept. As soon as his head was on the pillow he was taken in spirit to an exceedingly high mountain on which was a mighty precipice with jagged rocks on both sides and rough cliffs jutting out in varied ways. The one who was guiding him pushed him from the top of the ridge. He fell headlong over the rocks. He fell from ledge to ledge, hitting boulder after boulder until he reached the foot of the crag. All his limbs seemed shattered and his bones fractured.

While he was lying so shattered, he was bidden by his guide to get up, because there was still a long way to go. The friar replied: "You are a cruel and unreasonable man. You see me shattered to death and still bid me get up." The guide came up, touched him and immediately healed his broken limbs. And then he showed him a great plain with sharp rocks, thorns and

77

briars, with muddy and water bogs. He told the friar that he must walk barefoot across it till he came to the end of the plain where there was a fiery furnace seen from afar into which he must enter. When he had crossed that plain with much agony and had reached the furnace the angel said to him: "Go into that furnace. You must." "Alas," replied the friar, "what a heartless guide you are who, after seeing me racked with the torments of that agonizing plain, when I need nothing so much as rest, bid me enter that furnace." As he looked round it he saw devils standing everywhere with red-hot pitchforks with which as he hung back, they suddenly thrust him in. He had stepped into the fire and stood there for a while when the angel pushed him out of the furnace saying: "Prepare to go on, you still have a big danger to face." "Most cruel guide," said the friar, "who are moved by no compassion. You see that I am almost all burnt up and you bid me go on to a horrible danger." The angel touched and completely healed him. He led him to a bridge which he could not cross without the greatest peril. It was narrow and terribly slippery with a wild river flowing underneath full of serpents, reptiles, scorpions and toads, and horrific stench. "Cross that bridge," said the angel, "because you must." "How can I cross it," he asked, "without falling in so perilous a river?" The angel said: "Follow after me and put your foot where you see me put mine and you will cross in safety." That is what he did until they came to the middle of the bridge safely, when the angel left him, flying up to a wondrous building set on a very high hill. He saw clearly the angel fly there. He was left without a guide in the middle of the bridge and all those dreadful creatures lifted up their heads to devour him if he fell. He stood in such fear that he did not know what to do because he could neither turn back nor go forward. In such torture and peril he bent down and embraced the bridge, and seeing there was no refuge save in God, he began from his inmost heart to call on the Lord Jesus

Christ, that by his most holy and righteous mercy he would deign to help him. After this prayer he seemed to be sprouting wings. Rejoicing much at this he waited for them to grow, hoping to fly over to the place where the angel had flown.

He was in too great a hurry to fly because the wings had not grown enough; failing in flight he fell upon the bridge and all the feathers dropped from him. Thoroughly afraid, and again clasping the bridge, he tearfully begged Christ's mercy. Again he felt he was sprouting wings, and as before, in haste to fly before the wings had properly grown, he fell a second time on to the bridge, and all the feathers fell out. Observing that it was through haste that he was not able to fly properly, he said to himself: "If I sprout wings a third time, I shall wait long enough to be ready for flight." And it seemed a century and half or more went by between the three sproutings of wings. When he was convinced he had properly grown his wings, on this third occasion he flew boldly up to the building on the hill to which the angel had flown. When he reached the door of that lovely dwelling, the doorkeeper said to him: "Who are you who come here?" "I am a friar minor," he replied. "Wait till I bring Saint Francis," said the doorkeeper, "and see if he recognizes you."

While he was waiting, he looked closely at the walls of that marvellous city. They were of such transparency that everything which was done inside, and the wondrous choirs of the saints, were clear to see. And out came Saint Francis and Brother Bernard and Brother Giles, and behind Saint Francis such a multitude of saintly men and women of God who had followed in his steps that they seemed beyond numbering. Saint Francis said to the doorkeeper: "Let him in, because he is one of my brethren." He took him in and showed him many wondrous things. He immediately felt such sweetness and consolation that he forgot all the tribulations which had gone before as if he had never been in the world. Then Saint Francis said: "Son, you must return to the world and stay there seven days, during which prepare yourself as you may. Then I will come for you, and you will come with me to this wondrous place of the blessed."

Saint Francis wore a long stole adorned with many stars and his five stigmata were like very bright stars that gleamed with such light that they seemed to illumine the whole city with their beams. Brother Bernard had on his head a most beautiful crown of stars. Brother Giles was completely clad in wondrous light, and he recognized there many other friars minor with the blessed Francis, and there were many whom he had not seen. Taking leave unwillingly, the brother returned to the world as the brothers were ringing for prime. No more time had elapsed save that which lies between matins and dawn, though to him it seemed many years.

The brother related his vision to the warden, and within seven days he fell into a fever. On the seventh day Saint Francis came with a glorious company of saints and led to the place of the blessed the soul of that brother, purged in the vision related by the angel guide. To the praise and glory of Jesus Christ our Lord. Amen.

Chapter 30

How Brother Bernard remained from matins to nones rapt over the body of Christ.

WHAT MEASURE OF GRACE was shown by the All-Highest to the evangelical poor who of their own free will forsook all for the love of Christ, appeared in Brother Bernard of whom we have already told. After he had taken the habit of the holy father his mind was frequently enraptured up to God. Thus it happened on one occasion when he was in church hearing mass, with his mind fixed on God, that he became so absorbed and rapt, that at the elevation of the body of Christ, he perceived nothing, nor did he kneel or pull back his cowl as did the others. His eyes fixed and staring he stood there till nones. After nones he recovered crying out in a voice of wonder: "O brothers, O brothers, O brothers. There is nobody in this land so great or so noble, who if he were offered a palace full of gold would not willingly carry a sack of dung in order to acquire such a noble treasure." Towards this heavenly treasure, promised to those who love God, Brother Bernard was so uplifted in mind, that for fifteen years he continually went about with mind and face uplifted heavenwards. Because of this elevation of mind toward heavenly enlightenment and his complete absorption in divine favors, never in those fifteen years did he ever satisfy his hunger at table but would always eat a little of what was set before him, saying that abstinence is not concerned with what a man does or relishes; true abstinence lies in refraining from things that taste good. He thus attained such clarity of thought and intellectual perception that even high-ranking clerics had recourse to him. He was in great demand to explain obscure problems in any passage of the Scriptures.

For his mind was so completely abstracted from the things of this world, that like a swallow soaring to great heights, sometimes for twenty days, at other times for thirty, he would range alone over mountain tops completely absorbed in heavenly things. This is why Brother Giles used to say of him that to no other man had been vouchsafed the gift bestowed on Brother Bernard of Quintavalle, namely that of nourishing himself in flight like a swallow. Thanks to this outstanding favor he had from God, Saint Francis eagerly and frequently would talk with Brother

Bernard both day and night. Thus the two were frequently found rapt up to God together for a whole night in the woods where they met to talk of the Lord Jesus Christ.

Chapter 31

How the Devil appeared to Brother Ruffino in the form of Christ and told him he was damned.

BROTHER RUFFINO, ONE OF THE NOBLEST gentlemen of Assisi and a companion of Saint Francis, was at one time during the saint's lifetime strong assailed and tempted in his soul by the Devil concerning pre-destination. For the old Enemy kept putting into his heart that he was not among those predestined to eternal life and that what he was doing in the service of the Order was a waste of time. The result of this torment which went on for many days was that he became melancholy and depressed, and was ashamed to reveal his conflict to Saint Francis. Nevertheless he did not cease in any way from his accustomed prayers. So the old Enemy, intent on heaping trial upon trial, which so grievously afflicts the servants of God, added to his inward conflict by assailing him from without.

And so appearing to him in the form of the Crucified he said: "O Brother Ruffino, why do you torment yourself with prayer and penance, since you are not one of those predestined to eternal life? Take my word for it, for I know whom I have chosen. And do not believe the son of Peter Bernardone if he tells you the contrary; and do not question him on this matter, for neither he nor anyone else knows anything about it; but I, who am the son of God, do know.

Believe me therefore for certain, that you are numbered among the damned. Brother Francis himself is damned, as are you and his father; whosoever follows him is deceived."

Brother Ruffino's mind was so overclouded by the prince of Darkness that he lost faith in Francis and his love for him, and was unwilling to admit it to him. But what Brother Ruffino did not tell the holy father was revealed to him by the Spirit of the Lord. The holy father himself seeing in spirit the peril of Brother Ruffino sent Brother Masseo in his stead to persuade Ruffino to come to him. Now Brother Ruffino and Saint Francis were staying at the friary of Mount Subasio near Assisi. Brother Ruffino answered Brother Masseo thus: "What have I to do with Brother Francis?" Then Brother Masseo, a man full of the Holy Spirit, clearly recognizing the wiles of the malignant Enemy, said: "O Brother Ruffino, do you not know that Saint Francis is like an angel of God, who has enlightened so many souls in this world and from whom we too have received so many gifts of divine favor? And so my strong desire is that you should come to him, for I see clearly that you have been beguiled by the Devil." Immediately Brother Ruffino came to Saint Francis. And when Francis saw him from afar off he began to call out: "O Brother Ruffino, you poor fellow, whom have you believed?" And Brother Ruffino told him in detail of the temptations he had experienced both within and without. Francis then showed him that the one who had made those earlier suggestions was the Devil and not Christ, and that therefore he should in no way listen to his suggestions. "So when the Devil tells you you are damned, you should confidently reply: 'Apri la bocca et mote cecato,' that is, open your mouth and I shall excrete in it. And let this be a sign to you that he is the Devil; for when you have said those words he will immediately flee. By this you must realize that he was the Devil, because he had hardened your heart against every good thing—which is precisely his purpose. The blessed Christ never hardens the heart of man, he says rather: 'I shall take from you your heart of stone and give you a heart of flesh.'"

Brother Ruffino perceiving that Saint Francis was speaking of the whole succession of temptations that had tormented him within and without, began to weep most bitterly. He knelt before the saint and humbly confessed his fault in having concealed anything from him. He was totally comforted in God, thanks to the admonition of the holy father, and completely changed for the better. Then said Saint Francis: "Go, my son, to confession. Do not cease from your accustomed devotion to prayer, and be convinced that this temptation will prove a great help and consolation to you, as you will soon discover." Brother Ruffino returned to his cell in the woods to pray. And as he was praying bathed in tears, behold, the old Enemy appeared in the person of Christ saying: "Brother Ruffino, did I not tell you not to believe the son of Peter Bernardone, and since you are damned, not to persist in tearful prayers? What does it profit you if you torment yourself while you are still alive and are damned when you die?" Brother Ruffino immediately replied: "Apri la bocca et mote cecato."

The Devil departed discomfited amid a mighty commotion and a landslide of rocks on Mount Subasio. For a long time a stream of rocks hurtled down, where to this day an awesome pile of stones is still visible. Far down the valley of this mountain clashing rocks gave off mighty flashes of fire. Such was the terrible clatter of rocks that Saint Francis and his awestruck companions came out of the friary to gaze upon the strange sight. Brother Ruffino openly told them that it was the evil Enemy who had deceived him, then went back to Saint Francis and prostrating himself on the ground again confessed his fault. Comforted by Saint Francis he was completely reconciled.

Later on when he was praying amid copious tears, behold, the blessed Christ appeared to him, and soothed his soul totally with divine love saying: "You did well my son, to believe Brother Francis, for he who tormented you was the Devil. I am Christ your master, and that I may fully reassure you, let this be a sign to you: as long as you are in this wood you will never again be downcast." And Christ blessed Brother Ruffino and dismissed him in such joy, tranquillity of spirit and elevation of mind that night and day he remained absorbed in God. Thereafter he was so strengthened in grace, blessing and the certainty of eternal life, that he was changed into a totally different man. His mental uplift was so strengthened, as was his perseverance in continual prayer, that he would have remained within his limited circle of friends contemplating things of heaven day and night, if somebody had not prevented him.

And so Saint Francis used to say of him that Brother Ruffino was canonized in heaven by the Lord Jesus Christ while he was still alive, and that he himself would not hesitate to say (but not in his presence) that Saint Ruffino had been canonized in heaven though he was still on earth. To the praise of our Lord Jesus Christ.

Chapter 32

Of the strange obedience of Brother Ruffino, friend of the blessed Francis.

BROTHER RUFFINO AS THE RESULT of constant contemplation was so absorbed in God that he became almost insensible. He spoke very rarely, and was not endowed with any gift for spreading the Word, for he had not the courage to speak out. But one day Francis ordered Brother Ruffino to go to Assisi and to preach to the people whatever the All-Highest inspired him to say. But Brother Ruffino replied: "Reverend Father, forgive me, do not send me on this task, for as you know, I have no gift of speech; in fact I am a simple man and an uneducated ignoramus." But Saint Francis said: "Because you have not obeyed me instantly I order you, for obedience' sake, to go to Assisi naked, retaining only your breeches. Going into some church or other you shall preach to the people half clad."

Forthwith showing true obedience he made his way to Assisi and entered a church, having made his bow to the altar he stood up to preach. But the men and boys began to laugh and say: "Look, these fellows do so much penance that they become half-witted." But meanwhile Saint Francis, pondering on the prompt obedience of Brother Ruffino and on his own harsh order, began to reproach himself very grievously saying: "Whence comes the right to you, son of Peter Bernardone, miserable creature, to order Brother Ruffino who comes of the noblest citizens of Assisi, to go and preach to the people half clad? In God's name I shall see to it that you yourself shall experience what you command another man to do." So saying, in the fervor of the Holy Spirit he divested himself of his tunic and half clad made his way to Assisi, taking with him Brother Leo, who in very puzzled cogitation carried Brother Ruffino's tunic and that of his companion.

When the men of Assisi beheld him thus half clad they began to mock him as a crank, thinking that both he and Brother Ruffino were driven demented by their penance. But the blessed Francis found Brother Ruffino who had already begun to preach. Reproachfully he was saying: "O greatly beloved, shun this world and renounce sin; restore what is not yours if you wish to escape hell. Keep the commandments by loving God and your neighbor if you wish to reach heaven, and do penance, for the kingdom of heaven is at hand."

Thereupon Saint Francis went up into the pulpit and preached so impressively about contempt for the world, the holiness of penance, voluntary poverty, longing for the heavenly kingdom, nakedness and indignities suffered, and the most holy passion of our crucified Lord Jesus Christ, that all who had assembled there in great numbers, men and women, began to weep aloud. With unbelievable devotion and compunction they cried aloud to heaven for the mercy of the All-Highest, so much so that all fell into a state of mental daze.

And on that day in Assisi there was such weeping among the assembled multitude for the Passion of our Lord Jesus Christ as had never been heard in that city. And when the people had been thus uplifted, Christ's flock consoled, and the name of our Lord Jesus Christ loudly blessed, Saint Francis caused his brother to be reclothed, while he at the same time resumed his habit. And so reclad in their tunics and praising the Lord for having vanquished themselves and uplifted Christ's flock and shown how the world should be spurned, they returned to the friary of Porziuncula. Those who managed to touch the hem of his garment deemed themselves blessed. To the praise of our Lord Jesus Christ.

Chapter 33

How Brother Ruffino liberated a man possessed of the Devil.

THE AFORESAID BROTHER RUFFINO, because of the powerful concentration of his heart on God, and his angelic serenity of mind, whenever anybody spoke to him, would reply with such seriousness, gentleness, and waywardness of voice, that he seemed to be returning from a different world. On one occasion, called upon by his companions to go begging for bread, he replied in truly godlike manner: "Frater a te imo molto volontire: Brother, very willingly." On one occasion in fact, when he was begging for bread in the streets of Assisi, there appeared a man possessed by a devil, led along firmly bound, and guarded by several men, being taken to Saint Francis to be rid of the devil. Having caught sight of Brother Ruffino from a distance, he forthwith began to shout and rave so violently that he burst all his bonds and leapt clear of the hands of his captors. They for their part, amazed at such strange behavior, conjured him to tell them why his torment was worse than usual. The reply came: "Because yonder beggarly brother, that submissive, humble, and holy Brother Ruffino, consumes and tortures me with his saintly virtues and humble prayers. For that reason I cannot bear to remain in this man any longer." And with these words the devil immediately left him.

When Brother Ruffino heard this, and because these men and the restored sufferer showed him such respect, he gave praise and glory to God and the Lord

Jesus Christ, and exhorted them that in all such matters they should glorify God and the Savior Lord Jesus Christ who is for ever blessed. Amen.

Chapter 34

How Brother Ruffino saw and touched the wound in the side of Saint Francis.

THOSE SACRED WOUNDS that Christ the Son of God had miraculously imprinted on the hands, feet and side of our blessed father Francis he so carefully concealed from all eyes, that during the saint's lifetime, scarcely anybody ever managed to see them properly. For thereafter he never went about barefooted, and only the tips of his fingers were visible to his companions, for he concealed his hands in his sleeves, mindful of the words spoken by the angel to Saint Tobias: "A goodly thing it is to conceal a king's secret." The wound in his side especially he kept hidden during his lifetime, so that except for Ruffino, who by some dutiful effort earned the right to see it, nobody else managed to catch sight of it. But Brother Ruffino by a threefold experience convinced himself and others concerning the existence of a sacred wound in his side.

The first time was on one occasion when having to wash the holy father's hose, he discovered various blood-stains on the right-hand side. He thus ascertained for a certainty that this was blood flowing from a wound on the right-hand side. Whenever Saint Francis noticed that Brother Ruffino folded down the said garments in order to see the sign, he would reprimand him.

On another occasion, in order to be even more certain, Brother Ruffino while scraping down the holy father, thrust his finger into the wound itself—which caused Saint Francis in anguish to cry out loudly: "God forgive you, Brother Ruffino, why did you want to do that?"

On the third occasion the same brother desirous of seeing that venerable wound with human eyes said to Saint Francis with affectionate deference: "I beg you, father, to do me a very great favor: give me your habit, and in fatherly affection accept mine." This Brother Ruffino used to do in order that whenever Francis divested himself, he might actually behold with his own eyes the wound in his side that he had at one time touched with his hand and so it was. Thus Saint Francis, yielding to the affection of Brother Ruffino, divested himself of his own habit and accepted the other's habit; and since he possessed that one only, he could not cover himself while undressing and so prevent Brother Ruffino from closely observing the wound in question. Thus he was fully convinced concerning the sacred wound by these three proofs. To the praise and glory of our Lord Jesus Christ.

Chapter 35

How Brother Ruffino was one of three chosen souls.

JUST AS OUR BLESSED LORD JESUS CHRIST says in the Gospel: "I know my sheep and my sheep know me," so our blessed father Francis by divine revelation knew all the merits and virtues of his followers. And he knew equally well their shortcomings and their failings, and consequently had learnt how to provide the appropriate remedy for all, by humbling the proud and exalting the humble, by condemning vices and exalting virtues, as anybody can observe in the wonderful revelations he had concerning that original household of his.

To mention one example among many: Saint Francis was once sitting in a certain small friary with his companions exercising himself in talking with them about God. But Brother Ruffino, a man notably distinguished for his piety, was not on this occasion present with them for this holy discourse, because he had not yet returned from the woods where he had gone to pray. And as Saint Francis continued with his holy exhortations and divine conversations with the aforesaid followers, behold, there came forth from the woods where he had been contemplating heavenly things, and passed by not far from Saint Francis, Brother Ruffino, a noble citizen of Assisi, but an even nobler servant of God, the purest of unmarried men, uplifted by the noble privilege of divine contemplation, and moreover graced in the sight of God and man with the sweet-smelling flowers of fellowship.

When the saint beheld him from afar off he turned to his followers and said: "Tell me, beloved friends, who is the saintliest soul that God has in this world." They humbly replied that they considered that Saint Francis himself was distinguished by that privilege. But he replied: "I, beloved brethren, am the unworthiest and vilest man that God has in the world. But do you see Brother Ruffino yonder coming out of the wood? God has revealed to me that his soul is one of the three saintliest souls in this world. And this I tell you with conviction that I would not hesitate to call Ruffino himself a saint while he still lives in the body, since his soul is already confirmed in grace, sanctified and canonized in heaven by the Lord Jesus Christ."

Such in fact were the words used by the blessed Francis, but never in the presence of the said brother. In words he demonstrated that like a good shepherd he knew the shortcomings of his own sheep, as he showed in the case of Brother Elias when he upbraided him for pride; in the case of Brother John of Capella, when he prophesied to him that because of malice he would hang himself; in the case of a brother whose throat was clutched by the Devil when he was corrected for disobedience; and in the case of brothers coming from the Terra di Lavoro, when he reproved one of them for an offence committed against a travelling companion.

But he knew too of the good graces that abounded in his flock, as appears in the case of Brother Bernard, of the aforesaid Brother Ruffino and many others, concerning whom God revealed great things to the blessed Francis the good shepherd. To the praise of our Lord Jesus Christ.

Chapter 36

How Saint Francis converted two nobles from the March of Ancona while preaching at Bologna, namely Brother Peregrine and Brother Ricerio.

ON ONE OCCASION Saint Francis travelling abroad had reached Bologna. When the people heard of his arrival, there was such a universal concourse to meet him that he could scarcely make his way through the country. For all were desirous of seeing him as the flower of this world and the angel of God, so much so that only with the greatest difficulty was he able to reach the city square. To a mighty congregation of people therefore, of men, women, and many scholars, Saint Francis standing up in their midst, and at the prompting of the Holy Spirit, preached so miraculously and amazingly that he seemed not a man but an angel. For his heavenly words seemed to shoot like sharp arrows from the bow of divine wisdom; they penetrated the hearts of all so effectively that he converted a mighty crowd of men and women from a state of sin to tears of repentance.

Among them were scholars from among the nobler families of the Marches of Ancona, namely Peregrine of the house of Fallaro, and Ricerio of Muccia. These among others, deeply touched by the words of the holy father, came to the blessed Francis saying that they wished to forsake the world entirely and to adopt the habit of his friars. Saint Francis pondering on their fervor, perceived through the Holy Spirit that they had been sent by God. Moreover he realized to what kind of communal life each of them should commit himself. So welcoming them joyfully he said: "Do you, Peregrine, take the path of humility; and you, Ricerio, act as the servant of the brethren." And so it was; for Brother Peregrine never had any desire to be a priest but remained a lay brother, although he was well-educated and learned in canon law. Thanks to such humility he attained the greatest perfection of virtue and especially the grace of remorse and the love of our Lord Jesus Christ. Fired with the love of Christ and burning with a desire for martyrdom, he made his way to Jerusalem to visit the holy places of the Savior, taking with him a volume of the Gospels. And whenever he read about the places whence God and man had proceeded, touched them with his feet and beheld them with his eyes, he would bow down on the spot and embrace with his arms these most holy places of the faith and kiss them with loving lips. With tears of piety he so drenched everything that he stimulated to the utmost devotion all who beheld him.

In the obedience to God's ordinance, he returned to Italy, and as the real Peregrine of this world, and as a citizen of the heavenly kingdom, very rarely visited his blood relations. He would encourage them to despise the world and with serious words urge them to the love of God; then hurriedly and hastily he would withdraw from them saying that Jesus Christ who ennobles the soul, is not to be found among relatives and acquaintances.

About Brother Peregrine, Brother Bernard, the firstborn son of our holy Father Francis, had this very remarkable thing to say, namely, that Brother Peregrine was one of the most perfect men of this world. He was indeed a restless pilgrim (*peregrinator*); for the love of Christ that he ever retained in his heart did not permit him to find repose in any living creature, nor to fix his affection on anything temporal, but always prompted him to hasten back to the land of his birth, to rise from virtue to virtue until he transformed a loving person into a person beloved. Finally full of virtues and having worked many miracles before his death, he fell asleep in Christ, whom he loved with all his heart. To the praise of God and our Lord Jesus Christ.

Chapter 37

How Saint Francis freed Brother Ricerio from great temptation.

BROTHER RICERIO, ONE OF THE COMPANIONS of Brother Peregrine on earth, and now his fellow sojourner in heaven, made his way through an active life while he lived, and most faithfully serving both his

God and his neighbor, became a very close and beloved companion of Saint Francis. He thus learned a great deal from Saint Francis, and from his teaching clearly perceived the truth in many doubtful matters. He learned to know the will of God and following the prophecy of the holy father, was the servant of his brethren. He became minister of the Marches of Ancona, and as a result of his zeal for God that ever burned in his heart, governed the province with the greatest calm and discretion, following the example of Christ who preferred doing to preaching. But after some time divine ordinance exposed him to temptation—to the ultimate advantage of his soul— whereat over-anxious and distressed, he punished himself with fasting, scourgings, tears and prayers; but he could not free himself from temptation. He was frequently reduced to extreme despair, for the immensity of his temptation led him to think he was forsaken of God. Reduced indeed to the depths of desolation and despair, he pondered in his heart saying: "I will arise and go to my father Francis, and if he shows me affection, I believe that God will be merciful to me." And taking to the road he went to Saint Francis, but Saint Francis was lying grievously ill in the palace of the bishop of Assisi. As he pondered on God there was revealed to him by God the seriousness of the temptation, the arrival and the purpose of the said brother. At once he summoned his companions, namely Brother Masseo and Brother Leo, saying: "Go forth quickly to meet my son Ricerio; embrace him and greet him on my behalf, and tell him that among all the brethren in the world I love him especially." So they as true sons of obedience went forth immediately to meet Brother Ricerio. And when they found him, they embraced him, and as Saint Francis had instructed them quoted the loving words of the father, which so filled his soul with consolation, that he was completely melted with joy as it were.

What gladness he then showed, what transports of

joy, what praise and thanks he rendered to God for having blessed his journey could scarcely be expressed in words. "O kindly Jesus, who never forsakes those who trust in you, but always provides us in the face of temptation the means to enable us to bear it." What more remains to be said? He reached the place where lay that angelic and most holy man Francis, and although he was grievously ill, he arose and went to meet him. Embracing him he said: "Gentlest son, Brother Ricerio, among all the brethren in the world I love you." And imprinting the sign of the Cross on his brow, and very affectionately kissing him there he said: "My very dear son, this temptation was given you for your great profit, but you no longer need that advantage." Marvellous to relate, immediately all the diabolical temptation disappeared as if he had never felt it in his whole life, and he remained totally reconciled in God. To the praise of our Lord Jesus Christ.

Chapter 38

How Saint Francis appeared to Brother Leo.

FRANCIS, LOVER OF THAT GLORIOUS INNOCENCE that adds comeliness to the body and leads the soul on to grace and glory, for the sake of the great purity and dove-like innocence he perceived in Brother Leo, frequently treated him as a companion, and often admitted him to his own secrets both by day and by night. For this reason among all the companions of the holy father, the one who came to know the most about his secrets and wonders was the aforesaid Brother Leo. He frequently saw him elevated into the air, as will be told later. He frequently heard him speaking with Christ, the blessed Virgin and with angels. Moreover he saw a fiery light descending from heaven upon Saint Francis and heard a voice coming from the light itself speaking with him. One day too when they were walking along together he saw a most beautiful Cross going on ahead of the face of the holy father, with Christ hanging on it. And he observed that this miraculous Cross stopped whenever the saint stopped, and when he walked on, so did the Cross. Wherever Saint Francis made his way it went on before him. And the Cross was of such brightness that not only did it light up the face of Saint Francis, but it gave beauty to the air around about, and Brother Leo could distinguish everything by its clear light.

To Brother Leo, Saint Francis brought wondrous consolations in his lifetime, and even after his death appeared to him frequently. And so on one occasion when Brother Leo was watching and praying he appeared to him saying: "O Brother Leo, you recall that when I was in the world, I predicted that a mighty famine would come over the whole earth, and I said that I knew a certain miserably poor man whom God had spared because of his love for him; and that as long as that poor creature lived no scourge or famine would be sent." Brother Leo replied: "I well remember, most holy father." And Saint Francis said: "I was that creature, that miserably poor man for the love of whom God did not send famine upon mankind; but out of humility I was unwilling to reveal myself. Now know for certain, Brother Leo, that when I have departed from this world, there will come a terrible and all-embracing famine upon the earth so that many men will die of hunger." And so it proved, for about six months after he had uttered these words, such a mighty famine spread everywhere, that not only did men devour the roots of plants, but the bark of trees, and a vast number of men perished of hunger. From what has been said therefore, there emerges clearly the innocence of Brother Leo, the divine friendship of Brother Leo, Saint Francis and his awesome gift of prophecy. To the praise of our Lord Jesus Christ. Amen.

Chapter 39

Of Brother Leo, who saw Saint Francis elevated from the ground and felt his stigmata.

WHEN THE BLESSED FATHER FRANCIS began to experience God-given favors in that soul of his, he was frequently uplifted into the air, not only mentally but also physically. For in these elevations there worked a divine ordinance from God, in that the more pressingly he felt the gifts of divine grace, the higher he was uplifted from the ground, as his companions many times saw on the evidence of their own eyes, and strangely enough, as did Brother Leo, whom because of his dove-like, nay angelic innocence Saint Francis quite frequently permitted to share in his private preoccupation with prayer. Hence Brother Leo often had the privilege of seeing the holy father elevated into the air—to a greater or lesser height according to the degree of intensity of those celestial feelings thanks to which he was lifted up towards God as he progressed from virtue to virtue.

On one occasion Brother Leo saw Saint Francis elevated from the ground to the extent that he was able to touch his feet. On another occasion he had the privilege of seeing the saintly father raised up to the tree-tops; on another, carried upwards to such a height that human sight could scarcely discern him. Whenever he managed to reach the feet of the blessed

Francis he would embrace them, and kissing them with tears of the utmost devotion prayed saying: "God be merciful to me a sinner, and through the merits of this most holy man, grant that I may find thy most holy mercy." Whenever he saw him so lifted up that he was unable to touch him, he would prostrate himself beneath Saint Francis and utter a prayer similar to the previous one. These elevations of the holy father occurred at the friary of Alverna and at numberless other places.

To Brother Leo alone would Saint Francis submit his stigmata to be touched and to be revived with new fragments of twig, which he used to renew every day of the week, between those miraculous nails and the rest of his flesh, in order to restrain the blood and ease the pain. With the exception of Thursday and throughout Friday he would refuse the application of any relief, in order that for the love of Christ, on that day of crucifixion he might hang crucified along with Christ amidst the agonies of the Cross. Sometimes Saint Francis would place carefully those hands marked by their venerable stigmata against Brother Leo's heart. From this contact Brother Leo would feel such devotion in his heart that he almost expired, being reduced by constant sobbing to edifying unconsciousness. To the praise of our Lord Jesus Christ. Amen.

Chapter 40

The miracle of the holy stigmata of the blessed Francis.

HOW IMPRESSIVE WERE THOSE MIRACULOUS STIGMATA of the holy father becomes evident from a certain notable miracle clearly demonstrated at a certain friary of preaching brothers. For there present was a certain preaching brother who detested the blessed Francis so cordially that he could not bear to see him in a painting, nor hear about him, nor believe in his heart that he had been marked with the holy stigmata. And so when the said brother, from a community beyond the mountains, was stopping at the aforesaid friary in whose refectory there was a picture of Saint Francis, he secretly made his way thither, moved by distrust and dislike, and with a knife scraped off the stigmata from the painting of the holy father so that there remained no trace whatever.

But the following day when the same brother was sitting at table and again looked at the picture of Saint Francis, there he saw the stigmata in the places whence he had scraped them away, fresher than before. Ruefully he realized that he had not completely scraped them away in the first place, and watching for a moment when nobody would be about—for an evil-doer hates the light—he drew near and for a second time scraped away the saint's stigmata, in such a way, however, that he did not damage the underlying stone on which the picture was painted.

On the third day when the same brother was sitting at table, he turned round towards the picture of Saint Francis and behold! he beheld the stigmata looking beautiful and new, never had they looked so fresh. Then the same brother, shrouded in the darkness of iniquity and incited by perfidy, added a third sin to the second. In his heart he said: "In God's name, I will so destroy those stigmata that they will never appear again."

As his custom was, he waited for a moment when human eyes would not see him; but forgetting that all things are bare and open to the eyes of God, in a raging fury he took his knife and gouged out the signs of the stigmata from the painting, including the underlying stone. But he had no sooner finished his gouging than blood began to flow out; spurting forth strongly it proceeded to bloody the face, hands and habit of the said friar. In terror he fell down as if dead. The blood continued to flow and stream from the holy stigmata gouged out by that wretched man.

Meanwhile the brothers of the friary came upon him lying as if dead; realizing his wickedness they grieved greatly. Seeing that the blood continued to flow they stopped up the holes with pieces of rags, but were unable to staunch the flow. And so fearing that this would set laymen thinking, and that they themselves would suffer scandal and scorn, they devoutly considered having recourse to the blessed Francis. The prior, along with all the inmates of the priory, disrobed themselves before the picture of Saint Francis. Scourging one another, praying and weeping, they implored the blessed Francis to have pity and to forgive the offence of the said brother, and deign to staunch the flow of blood. And forthwith, thanks to their humility, the blood ceased to flow, and the stigmata remained in all their former beauty, to be venerated by all. From then on the aforesaid brother became an exceedingly devoted follower of Saint Francis; and as the brethren of the friary of Alverna have testified, that brother went up to Mount Alverna to say his devotions, took some blood-stained cotton with him and gave it to the brethren. After completing his devotions he also came to Saint Mary of the Angels and visited all the friaries of Saint Francis with great reverence and weeping. For wherever he could find anything concerning the doings of Saint Francis or his relics, he would break into such devout tears that he caused others to weep too. He also related the story of all the aforementioned miracles in the presence of many friars minor at Alverna and Assisi, but not in the presence of his own companions, lest by chance they should reckon the said miracles to the discredit of their order. By the merits of Saint Francis this brother became so attached to his companions, that sometimes not in their presence, yet strengthened by the love of God, he revered them with feelings of brotherly love. To the praise of our Lord Jesus Christ.

Chapter 41

How Christ appeared to Brother Masseo of Marignano, companion of the blessed Francis.

THOSE HOLY COMPANIONS of our blessed father Francis, poor in material things but enriched in God, did not seek to become wealthy in gold or silver, but strove most earnestly to be enriched with holy virtues by which we attain the virtues of everlasting life. So it happened one day that Brother Masseo, one of the chosen companions of the holy father, was present when they were discussing God. One of them said: "There was a certain friend of God who enjoyed the favor of an active contemplative life. And with these favors he attained such a depth of profound humility, that it made him think himself a very great sinner. This humility sanctified him, strengthened him and caused him constantly to grow in these graces, and better still, never allowed him to fall away from God."

When Brother Masseo heard these wonderful things and realized that here lay a treasure of life and eternal salvation, he became so fired with a desire to possess the virtue of such humility, so worthy of God's embrace, that with mighty fervor raising his face heavenwards, he bound himself with a mighty vow never to allow himself to exult in this world until he felt the presence of that perfect humility in his own soul. Having made this vow with holy intent he remained constantly in the seclusion of his cell, tormenting himself continually the while with unspeakable groanings to God; for it seemed to him that he was a man who richly deserved hell unless he attained that most holy humility that caused that friend of God of whom he had heard, although endowed with all virtues, to deem himself inferior to all others and richly deserving of hell. And while the unhappy Brother Masseo remained for many days hungry, thirsty, afflicting himself with weeping, it happened one day that he went into the woods. As he passed through, in his mighty fervor he kept uttering mournful cries and tearful sighs, begging the Lord to grant him that favor. And because the Lord heals those who are contrite and hearkens to the voice of the humble, there came to him a voice from heaven calling him twice: "Brother Masseo! Brother Masseo!" He recognizing the voice, thanks to the Holy Spirit, replied: "My Lord!" And the Lord replied: "What are you willing to give, what are you willing to give to possess this favor?" And Brother Masseo replied: "The eyes of my head." And the Lord said: "It is my wish that you have your eyes as well as the favor."

Brother Masseo remained so filled with the grace of his longed-for humility in the light of God, that he was constantly elated and frequently when he was praying he would indulge in discreet jubilation and in a subdued voice would imitate a dove with "Oo-oo-oo" and with cheerful and joyful countenance would give himself up to contemplation. He also became extremely humble, reckoning himself the least among all men.

Brother James of Falterone of sacred memory asked him why he did not change the manner of his rejoicing. He replied joyfully that when all that is good is found in one thing, it is not necessary to change one's manner. To the praise of our Lord Jesus Christ.

Chapter 42

How Saint Clare was taken on Christmas Eve to the Church of Saint Francis.

WHEN THE MOST DEVOUT CLARE, spouse of Christ in fact and in name, was gravely ill in body and nearing the end of her stay at San Damiano, she was unable to go with others to church to observe the canonical hours. At the approach of the celebration of the Nativity of our blessed Lord Jesus Christ, when the sisters were accustomed to go to matins and to take solemn communion at the mass of the Nativity, the blessed Clare, being seriously ill, remained behind alone, while all others went to the celebration, in no little distress at not being able to participate in such solemn celebrations.

But the Lord Jesus, wishing to console his most faithful spouse, let her attend the Church of Saint Francis in spirit for matins, for mass and for all the festive celebrations. Thus she heard perfectly the singing of the brothers and the playing of the organ right to the end of the mass, and what is more, she received holy communion and was fully consoled.

When the sisters came back to Saint Clare after the completion of the office in San Damiano, they said: "Dearest Lady Clare, what great comfort we have had at the Nativity of the Savior Lord; if only you could have been with us!" But she replied: "My dearest sisters and daughters: I thank God and my blessed Jesus Christ that I was consoled and did attend all the ceremonies of this holy night, but greater ones and more solemn ones than you attended. For by the grace of my Lord Jesus Christ and thanks to the care of my most blessed Saint Francis, I was present at the Church of Saint Francis, and with my own ears, bodily and spiritual, I heard all the chanting and the organ-playing. Moreover I received holy communion. Rejoice therefore at so great a favor shown to me, and praise Jesus Christ with all your hearts, because as I lay here sick I was present, as I have said—I know not how, whether bodily or translated—at the whole ceremony at the Church of Saint Francis." To the praise of the Lord Jesus Christ.

Chapter 43

How Saint Clare at the bidding of the Pope miraculously imprinted the Cross on loaves of bread.

SAINT CLARE, A MOST DEVOUT DISCIPLE of the Cross and a valued offshoot of Saint Francis, was of such sanctity that not only bishops and cardinals but even the Pope had an appreciative desire to see and hear her, and frequently visited her personally. In fact the Pope on one occasion came to Saint Clare's monastery in order to listen to heavenly and divine conversation with one who was a shrine of the Holy Spirit. Thus together they discussed at length the salvation of the soul and the praise of God. Saint Clare meanwhile ordered loaves of bread to be set out on all the tables for the sisters, desiring to keep loaves that had been blessed by the Vicar of Christ.

When the holy conversation was ended, kneeling with great reverence, she desired the Pontiff to be good enough to bless the loaves set before him. The Pope replied: "Most faithful Sister Clare, it is my wish that you should bless these loaves and make over them the sign of the blessing of Christ, to whom you have offered yourself as a rich sacrifice." But she replied: "Most holy father, excuse me, for in so doing I would be excessively blameworthy if in the presence of the Vicar of Christ, I a worthless female presumed to perform such a blessing." The Pope replied: "That it may not be imputed to presumption, but that in fact you may have the credit of so doing, I bid you in sacred obedience, make the sign of the Cross over these loaves and bless them in the name of our Lord Jesus Christ." Thereupon as an obedient daughter she very devoutly made the sign of the Cross over the loaves and blessed them. Marvellous indeed! for immediately on all the loaves there appeared a very beautiful sign of the Cross.

Some of the loaves were consumed with great devotion, some kept for the future as signs of a miracle. The Pope likewise filled with wonder at the miraculous Cross made by the spouse of Christ first gave thanks to God and then bestowed his comforting blessing on the blessed Clare.

There was staying at the monastery Ortolana,

mother of Saint Clare and Sister Agnes, her sister, all filled with the Holy Spirit, along with many other holy nuns and spouses of Christ, to whom Saint Francis sent many sufferers. By virtue of the Cross which they worshipped with their whole heart, as many as were touched by it went away cured. To the praise and glory of our Lord Jesus Christ.

Chapter 44

How the Lady Jacoba of Settesoli visited Brother Giles.

DURING THE STAY of the saintly Brother Giles in Perugia the Lady Jacoba of Settesoli, a noble lady very devoted to the friars minor, came to see him. A later arrival was Brother Gerardino of the Order of Minors, a very spiritually minded man who came in order to hear some edifying word from him. In the presence of several other friars Brother Giles said in his vernacular: "As a consequence of what a man has the ability to do, he does something he does not want to do."

In order to encourage Brother Giles to speak further Brother Gerardino said: "I am amazed, Brother Giles, that a man as a consequence of what he is able to do, should do something that he does not want to do, since a man by himself can do nothing. And this I can prove in several ways: firstly, ability presupposes something. Therefore what that something can do corresponds to its nature—just as fire warms because it is hot. But man of himself is nothing. That is why the apostle said: "Whosoever thinks himself something when he is nothing, deceives himself." So he who is nothing can accomplish nothing. Secondly, in this way I can prove that man can accomplish nothing; because if he can accomplish anything it is by reason of his soul alone, by reason of his body alone, or by reason of both together. If it is by reason of the soul only, it is certain that he can accomplish nothing, because the soul without the body cannot win merit nor lose it. If it is by reason of the body only he can accomplish nothing, because the body without the soul is void of life or form and therefore cannot act, because all action is form. If it is by reason of both jointly, then man is powerless, because if he could accomplish anything it would be by reason of the soul which is its form; but as has already been said, if the soul bereft of body can accomplish nothing, it can achieve much less if it is joined to the body, for "A perishable body weighs down the soul" (Wisdom 9:15). And of this I give you an example, Brother Giles: if a donkey cannot walk without a burden, much less can it do so with a burden. From this example therefore it is clear that the soul can accomplish less when burdened with the body than when free of it; but without the body it can accomplish nothing; therefore conjoined with it, it cannot accomplish anything either."

And many such arguments, some twelve in number—more than those mentioned—did he advance against Brother Giles in order to encourage him to speak; at which arguments all those who heard them were filled with admiration. Brother Giles retorted thus: "What you have been saying is unsound; admit you are wrong in all of it." Brother Gerardino smiling admitted his fault, but Brother Giles, perceiving that his admission was not sincere, said: "This confession, Brother Gerardino, is worthless; and when a confession is worthless, there remains nothing to be gained from it." And so saying he went on: "Can you sing, Brother Gerardino? Then sing with me!" And Brother Giles drew out from his sleeve a lyre with millet-stems for strings such as boys are used to making, and proceeding over the strings of the instrument, he went on in rhythmic words to annul and refute all twelve arguments. Beginning with the first proposition he said: "I am not speaking of man's being before creation, Brother Gerardino, for then it is true that he was nothing and could do nothing; but I am speaking of man after creation, to whom God gave free will to acquire merit by consenting to good works, and to earn discredit by refraining from them. For that reason your words were fallacious and misled me, Brother Gerardino, because the apostle Paul does not speak about the lack of substance, nor about the lack of ability, but about the lack of merit; as he says elsewhere, "If I have not love, I am nothing." Further, I was not speaking about a soul released or of a dead body, but about a living man, who by conforming to grace can do good if he so chooses; and by resisting grace does evil, which is nothing else but forsaking good. When you assert that "a perishable body weighs down the soul," Scripture does not mean thereby that it does away with the free will of the soul by which a man is able to do good or evil; it means that feelings and intelligence are prevented from operating and that the soul's memory is taken up with temporal matters. That is why in the same place Scripture continues: "this earthly tent burdens the thoughtful" (Wisdom 9:15) because that does not allow the soul to think freely and seek for the things that are above, where Christ is sitting at the right hand of God. So that the keenness of the powers of the soul, because of its multifarious occupations and because of the potentialities of the earthly body, is obstructed in many ways; that is why your words were misleading, Brother Gerardino."

In like manner he refuted all the other arguments,

so that Brother Gerardino apologized sincerely and admitted that a creature could accomplish something. Brother Giles went on: "Repentance is no good." Then he said: "Do you want me to demonstrate to you more clearly that a creature can accomplish something?" So getting up on to a chest he shouted out in a terrifying voice; "O damned soul, lying in hell." Then in a mournful voice he himself replied, as from the person damned in a manner that terrified everybody: "Woe, alas! woe! woe!" he shouted and wailed. Then Brother Giles spoke: "Tell us, wretched creature, why you went to hell," and the reply came: "Because the evil I could have avoided I did not shun, and the good I could have done I neglected to do." Then Brother Giles put the question: "What would you be willing to do if time for repentance were granted you, O damned captive?" And he replied, speaking for himself: "I would gradually put the whole world behind me in order to escape eternal punishment; for the world will come to an end but my damnation endures for eternity." Then turning to Brother Gerardino Brother Giles said: "Do you hear, Brother Gerardino, that a creature can accomplish anything?" Then he added: "Gerardino, tell me, when a drop of water falls into the sea, whether it gives its name to the sea or whether the sea gives its name to the drop?" Gerardino replied that both the substance and the name of the drop are absorbed and take on the name of the sea.

So saying Brother Giles, before the gaze of all there present, fell into a rapture. For he realized that human nature, in submission to divine nature, like the drop of water, was absorbed into the mighty ocean of Divinity by the incarnation of our Lord Jesus Christ, who is blessed for ever and for ever. Amen.

Chapter 45

How, when Brother Giles said "Virgin before childbirth," "Virgin in childbearing," and "Virgin after childbirth" three lilies arose.

DURING THE LIFETIME of the saintly Brother Giles there was a certain master of the Order of Preachers who for many years suffered serious doubt concerning the virginity of the Mother of Jesus Christ; for it seemed to him impossible that a mother could also be a virgin. But as a man of true faith he was greatly distressed over such doubts and desired to be freed from them by some enlightened men. Hearing that Brother Giles was a very enlightened man he went to him.

Holy Brother Giles with spiritual foreknowledge of his arrival, his purpose, and his mental conflict, went out to meet him. Before he reached him he smote the ground with a staff he carried in his hand and said: "O brother preacher, 'Virgin before childbirth.'" And immediately there came up on the spot he had struck with his staff a lily of surpassing beauty. Striking a second time he said: "O brother preacher, 'Virgin in childbirth!'" And there rose up another lily. Striking for the third time he said: "O brother preacher, 'Virgin after childbirth!'" And forthwith arose a third lily, whereupon Brother Giles fled. The brother preacher was immediately freed from his temptations and from then onwards always showed devotion towards holy Brother Giles.

Chapter 46

Of the marvellous revelation that occurred
in the hearts of Brother Giles and Saint Louis,
King of France.

WHEN SAINT LOUIS, KING OF FRANCE, had decided on
a seven-year pilgrimage to the holy places, he had
heard of the reputed sanctity of holy Brother Giles,
and set his heart on paying him a personal visit. So on
his pilgrimage he made a detour to Perugia where he
had heard that Brother Giles was living. Arriving at the
friars' gate as a miserably poor and unknown pilgrim
accompanied by a few companions, he urgently
enquired for Brother Giles. The gatekeeper went and
told Brother Giles that some pilgrim or other was
enquiring for him at the gate. He immediately
recognized in his heart who it was; and issuing forth
from his cell as if intoxicated he ran swiftly to the gate.
In wonder they rushed to embrace each other,
exchanging kisses of affection and kneeling together
as if they had known each other through long years of
friendship. Showing such signs of affectionate
friendship, uttering not a word to each other but
preserving absolute silence, they went their separate
ways.

But when Saint Louis was leaving, one of his
companions questioned by the brothers who it was
who had rushed to embrace Brother Giles so affectionately, replied that it was Louis, King of France,
who in the course of his pilgrimage had desired to see
the saintly Brother Giles. Querulously the friars said:
"Brother Giles, why were you so unwilling to say

anything to such a great king who came from France to see you and to hear some word of comfort?" Brother Giles replied: "Beloved brethren, do not be surprised if neither of us managed to say anything to each other, for the moment we embraced, the light of divine wisdom revealed his heart to me and mine to him. As we stood in the mirror of eternity, whatever he had intended to say to me, or I to him, we heard without sound from lips or tongue to our complete consolation, better than if we had spoken with our lips; for if we had tried to explain with the help of our voices what we felt within ourselves our words would have led to distress rather than to comfort. So be assured that he departed wondrously consoled."

Chapter 47

A certain wonderful piece of advice on the state of rapture that Brother Giles gave to Brother James.

BROTHER JAMES OF MASSA, a holy man and a layman, kept company with Saint Clare and many of the companions of Saint Francis. As a very devout man who enjoyed the grace of rapture, he wished to take counsel of Brother Giles and asked for permission to consult him how he should conduct himself when he experienced such grace. "Neither add to it nor take away from it; and shun crowds as much as you can," said Brother Giles. "What does that mean? Explain to me, Reverend Father." He replied: "When the mind is ready to be introduced into that most glorious light of God's goodness, it should neither have the presumption to add, nor be so careless as to diminish; it should love solitude as much as possible in order that the grace may be safeguarded." To the praise of our Lord Jesus Christ.

Chapter 48

How Saint Antony in preaching was clearly understood by men of different tongues.

THAT WONDERFUL VESSEL OF THE HOLY SPIRIT Saint Antony of Padua, one of the chosen disciples of blessed Francis, whom Saint Francis used to call his bishop, was preaching in the presence of the Pope and cardinals, in a gathering where there were Greeks and Latins, Frenchmen and Teutons, Slavs and Englishmen and many others of divers tongues. Inspired by the Holy Spirit and fired with the eloquence of the apostles, he poured forth mellifluous words, and all those present—men of different languages who heard him clearly and distinctly and with perceptive understanding—he filled with such sustained wonder and devotion that it seemed like a repetition of that ancient miracle of the apostles. In amazement they asked: "Is this man not a Spaniard? And how is it we all hear him speak in our own language in which we were born, Greeks and Latins, Slavs and Englishmen, Lombards and barbarians?"

The Pope too, amazed at the profound knowledge of the Holy Scriptures shown by Saint Antony, said: "Truly this man is the Ark of the Covenant and the treasure of the Holy Scriptures." Such were the companions our leader Francis won over, who along with his venerable associates could so nurture not only Christ's flock but also the Vicar of Christ, with the riches of the Holy Spirit, and supply them with heavenly weapons against the wiles of the enemy. To the praise of our Lord Jesus Christ who is blessed for ever and for ever. Amen.

Chapter 49

How Saint Antony by preaching to fishes converted many heretics to the faith.

OUR BLESSED LORD JESUS CHRIST, wishing to demonstrate how great was the sanctity of his most loyal servant Saint Antony, how devoutly his preaching and sound doctrine should be listened to, rebuked the folly of infidels and of ignorant heretics by means of irrational animals, fishes in fact, just as the she-ass rebuked the ignorance of Balaam.

For once when the blessed Antony was in Rimini where there was a large number of heretics, desirous of bringing them back to the light of the true faith and to the way of truth, he preached to them for many days about the Holy Scriptures. But they showed stony obstinacy and not only scorned his holy discourses but also refused to give him a hearing. So Saint Antony, under the Lord's inspiration, one day betook himself to the mouth of a river alongside the sea, and standing on a bank between the sea and the river began in the Lord's name to summon the fishes as to a sermon saying: "Hearken, O fishes of the sea and river, to the word of God that faithless heretics scorn to hear."

And behold! there immediately gathered before

Saint Antony so great a multitude of fish, great and small, the like of which had never been seen in those parts, all holding their heads just a little bit above water. There you would have seen big fish clinging closely to smaller fish, smaller ones quietly swimming under the fins of larger ones and staying there. You would even have seen the different species of fish hastening to join their fellows, and ranging themselves in the saint's presence like a field painted and wonderfully adorned with a variety of colors. You would have seen shoals of great fish like the serried ranks of an army, vying for places to hear the sermon. There you would have seen medium-sized fish taking up positions in the middle, as if instructed by the Lord, and remaining quietly in their places. There you would have seen a dense and numerous crowd of small fishes everywhere hastening like pilgrims to receive forgiveness, and approaching closer to the holy father as if under his protection. Thus in this divinely ordained sermon there were ranged, in order to hear Saint Antony, first the smaller fishes, next the middle-sized and thirdly, where the water was deeper, the largest fishes. And so to them in their ordered places Saint Antony solemnly began to preach saying: "O fish, my brothers, within your modest limits you should indeed give thanks to your Creator who for your inhabitation has provided such a noble element, so that you have fresh or salt water according to your need. Besides he has provided for you plenty of places for shelter that you may avoid the inclemencies of the weather. He has provided you with a clear transparent element, ways to get about and food to live on. Necessary foods a benign Creator prepares for you, even in the depths of the ocean.

"At the creation of the world you received from God with his blessing his command to multiply. During the Flood while other animals perished, you were preserved unharmed. Adorned and strengthened with fins you can roam wherever you please. It was granted to you by God's command to preserve Jonah the

116

prophet of the Lord, and after three days to restore him to dry land unhurt. You offered tax-money to the Lord Jesus Christ when in his poverty he had not the wherewithal to pay a stater. You had the distinction of providing food for the everlasting king, the blessed Lord Jesus Christ, before his resurrection. For all these reasons you are greatly bound to praise and bless the Lord, you who have already so many outstanding blessings ahead of other animals."

At these words and at similar exhortations some fish gave voice, some opened their mouths and all bowed their heads, by which signs they were able to praise the All-Highest. Uplifted in spirit at this reverence shown by the fishes Saint Antony, crying out in a very loud voice, said: "Blessed be the Everlasting God, that fishes of the sea honor God more than heretics do and that creatures lacking the power of reason hearken better than faithless men!"

The longer Saint Antony preached the more the throng of fishes increased; none of them moved away from the places they had occupied. At this miracle the people of the city flocked together as did the heretics aforementioned. When they beheld such an unusual miracle, so rightly to be wondered at since it was brute creatures who were listening to Saint Antony, they were filled with compunction; all sat down at the feet of Saint Antony that he might preach to them. Thereupon Saint Antony opening his mouth preached so wonderfully about the Catholic faith that he converted all the heretics present, and the faithful he sent away with his blessing, rejoicing and strengthened in their faith. The fishes too he dismissed all joyous and exultant; amid wonderful gambols and nods of satisfaction they departed to their various parts of the ocean.

For many days thereafter by his preaching and with the devotion of clerics Saint Antony reaped a mighty harvest in the conversion of heretics. To the praise of our Lord Jesus Christ who is for ever blessed. Amen.

Chapter 50

How Brother Conrad of Offida converted a certain young man and after death freed him from Purgatory.

BROTHER CONRAD OF OFFIDA, a wonderful zealot of the Gospel rule of our father Saint Francis, led such an intensely religious life and of such merit in the sight of God, that both in life and in death the Lord Jesus Christ repeatedly honored him. For when he was still alive and had come to the friary of Offida as a visitor, the brothers asked him for the love of God to admonish a certain youthful friar who acted in so childish and undisciplined a manner that he greatly upset both the young and old members of the community, and cared little or nothing about canonical hours and other regular practices. So Brother Conrad, out of compassion for this youth and other friars who were greatly disturbed on his account, humbly acceding to their prayers summoned him. Out of the bowels of charity he spoke inspired words of such effect that immediately the hand of God was laid upon the youth, and from a boy he became a mature man, so obedient, thoughtful and devout, so peace-loving, submissive, and so intent upon all good works, that just as before the whole community was upset by him, so afterwards they all rejoiced in his complete conversion to virtue, and bore him affection as to an angel. A few days after this conversion he fell ill and departed this world, at which the friars grieved greatly. After his death when Brother Conrad, who had converted him, was standing one night in prayer

118

before the altar of the friary, behold, his soul appeared before Brother Conrad, devoutly greeting him as father. He asked: "Who are you?" The reply was: "I am the soul of the youth lately deceased." Said Conrad: "My son, what is the matter?" The reply: "Dearly beloved father, by the grace of God and your instruction I am well because I am not damned; nevertheless because some of my sins were not fully expiated because of the short time I had, I am enduring mighty pains in Purgatory. So I beg you, father, that just as you came to my aid in my lifetime with your compassion, that you will deign to help me now in my sufferings, and say some Our Fathers for me, because your prayers are greatly acceptable to God."

Brother Conrad readily agreed and said one *Pater noster* together with *Requiem aeternam*. This done, the soul said: "O holy father, how this has helped me! I beg you to say it for me again." And when he had said it a second time the soul said: "Holy father, as you pray, I am completely relieved, I beg you not to cease praying." Brother Conrad realizing the soul was being helped by his prayers, recited one hundred Our Fathers for him. Whereupon the soul said: "On behalf of our Lord Jesus Christ I give thanks to you. May he grant you an everlasting reward for this kindness, because thanks to your prayers I am freed from all torture, and now I go to the glory of paradise." And with these words he went on his way to the Lord. Brother Conrad, in order to rejoice the brethren, related in order all that had happened that night. Both he and the others were greatly consoled. To the praise of our Lord Jesus Christ.

Chapter 51

How Brother John of Alverna was caught up in the infiniteness of God.

WHEN BROTHER JOHN HAD COMPLETELY renounced the consolations of this world, he was concerned to be consoled in God alone. And so whenever special solemn celebrations of our blessed Lord Jesus Christ came round, he would contrive for himself with divine favor, fresh consolations and marvellous revelations. So it fell out that as the Nativity of our Savior Lord approached, he awaited in all confidence consolation from the compassion of the blessed Christ. But the Holy Spirit that knows how to bestow gifts as it sees fit, at its own time and place, "so it depends not upon man's will or exertion, but upon God's mercy" (Romans 9:16), revealed to Brother John not the consolation he expected from the compassion of Christ but such a burning love from the love of Christ, that it seemed to him that his soul was snatched from his body. For a hundred times more fiercely than if he were in a furnace his heart and soul were aflame. As a consequence of this heat he panted in distress and in violent torment cried out aloud; because of the excessive fervor of his love and the force of the spirit he could not help calling out.

At the moment when he felt such intensity of love, the hope of salvation so fortified him that he did not believe that if he had died then, he would pass through Purgatory. And this great love persisted, although intermittently, for half a year, so that it seemed to breathe forth the spirit continuously.

Thereafter he had visitations and consolations innumerable, as I myself many times personally witnessed and as several others frequently investigated. For thanks to the excessiveness of his fervor and love, he was unable to conceal the visitations: in my presence he was several times enraptured. One night he was uplifted in such wondrous light that in the Creator he saw all created things, both heavenly and earthly, and all things set out and separated by differences of degree. He saw in fact how the choirs of blessed spirits rank below God, as does the earthly paradise and the blessed compassion of Christ. And the habitations of the lower orders he similarly perceived; he saw and felt that all things were evidence of a Creator. Later on God uplifted him above every creature so that his soul was absorbed and taken up into the infinite space of godliness and light, plunged into the sea of eternity and the infiniteness of God; so much so that he was conscious of nothing created or formed, nothing completed, nothing imaginable that human heart could conceive or tongue recount. And his soul was absorbed in that infinity of godliness, that ocean or that appearance of light, so that his very soul itself expanded as does a drop of wine in the depths of the sea; so that just as he found nothing in himself except ocean, so his soul saw nothing but God in all things, above all things, within all things, and beyond all things, and so three persons in one God and one God in three persons.

And he was conscious of eternal love that was responsible for the incarnation of the Son of God through that obedience to the Father by which he was incarnate. So along that way of incarnation and passion of the Son of God, meditating on it, bearing his burden and weeping, he reached that brilliance indescribable; for by no other way can the soul enter the presence of God than through Christ who is "the way, the truth and the life" (John 14:6).

121

There was also revealed to him in the same vision through Christ, whatever had happened, from the Fall of the first man, to the entry into eternal life of Christ who is the head and chief of all the chosen from the beginning of the world, and shall be unto the end, as was foretold by the holy prophets. To the praise of our Lord Jesus Christ. Amen.

Chapter 52

How Brother John saw Christ in glory in the Host, and how Christ stood on the altar when he said: "This is my body."

TO THE SAME BROTHER JOHN there happened a miracle worthy of being solemnly recorded as recounted by those who were present. When the aforesaid Brother John was staying at the friary of Mogliano in the custody of Fermo in the province of the Marches, on the first day after the octave of Saint Lawrence, that is, within the octave of the Assumption of the Blessed Virgin Mary, he rose before the time for matins and with the mighty unction of grace wherewith he had been prepared by the Lord, he said matins along with the brothers. After saying matins he proceeded into the garden; for he was conscious of such tremendous sweetness and gentleness that he appreciated in proportion to the mighty grace derived from those words of the Lord "*Hoc est corpus meum*" (This is my body), that he shouted out aloud, and in his heart kept on saying: "This is my body." Enlightened as to these words by the Holy Spirit, he beheld the blessed Christ along with the blessed

Virgin and a throng of angels and saints. And he understood those words of the apostle that "We are all one body in Christ, each one is a member one of another, that you may be able to comprehend with all the saints what is the breadth, the length, the height and the depth" and to know the love of Christ that passes all knowledge—all of which is included in the lofty sacrament that is celebrated when the words "This is my body" are uttered.

And when dawn broke, prompted by divine grace he entered the church, inspired by the fervor of the Holy Spirit, and thinking he was not heard by anybody— although a certain monk was in the choir and did hear him. Upset by the very magnitude of the grace granted him, he could not help giving three mighty shouts.

When therefore he went up to the altar to celebrate mass, which he was supposed to sing, his fervor grew more intense, and his love of Christ increased. There was granted to him a certain ineffable and incalculable sense of God's presence, which could not be explained in words. Fearing lest this feeling and miraculous fervor should increase so much that he would have to break off his mass, he knew not what to decide— whether to proceed or to wait.

However, as he had once had a similar experience and God had so restrained him that he had not interrupted his mass, somehow he felt confident to be able to proceed. Nevertheless he feared the consequences, for such infusions of divine power do not lie under man's control. When therefore he had proceeded as far as the Preface to the blessed Virgin, the illumination and sweetness of grace so intensified that when he came to "*Qui pridie*" (Who the night before he suffered), he could scarcely endure such sweetness and satisfaction. Having reached "This is my body," he kept repeating "*Hoc est . . . Hoc est . . .* This is . . . This is . . ." over and over again, and was unable to get further, for he was so conscious of the divine presence and of a throng of angels and saints, that he almost came to a halt because of the exaltation he felt in his soul.

So the warden of the friary, rushing to the aid of the distressed man, took his stand beside him, as did a friar behind him holding a lighted candle. Meanwhile the other friars stood there in fear along with many other men and women, with whom were other prominent women of the province, all of them in fearful expectation and weeping as women do. But Brother John, as if transported by this most blessed and blissful joy, stood still without completing the holy Consecration, because he felt that the Lord Jesus Christ was not entering into the Host, or rather that the Host was not being transubstantiated into the body of Christ until he added the words "*Corpus meum*" (My body). Unable to bear the majestical greatness of the Sacred Head, that is, of Christ as the paradise of the mystical body of Christ was revealed to him, he exclaimed "*Corpus meum.*" And immediately the form of the bread vanished and there appeared the Lord Jesus Christ incarnate and glorified, who revealed to him the humbleness that led to his incarnation and caused him daily to come into the hands of the priest. And that humility held Brother John in such bliss and ineffable and unutterable wonder, that he was unable to complete the words of the Consecration. For so wonderful is the humility and favor of our Savior toward us, as Brother John himself said, that the body cannot endure it or words explain it. This was why he was unable to go on. And so having said "*Hoc est corpus meum*—This is my body," he was transported into ecstasy and fell backwards, but was held up by the warden standing beside him lest he fall to the ground. There was a rush from the friars and other men and women in the church, and he was carried into the sacristy as if dead. His body had turned cold like the body of a dead man, and the fingers of his hands were so stiffly contracted that they could

124

scarcely be separated or moved. So he lay there as if lifeless from morning till the third hour, for it was summer time. I who witnessed all this desired very much to know what mercy of the Savior had worked upon him. As soon as he had recovered I went up to him and asked him for the love of God to be good enough to tell me what had happened. He having complete confidence in me, by the grace of God told me all, adding that while he was fulfilling his function and even before, his body was melted like strongly heated wax; his body felt boneless so that he could hardly raise his hands or make the sign of the Cross over the Host. He added that before he became a priest it was revealed to him that he was destined so to faint at mass, but because he had read many masses and the prophecy had not come to pass he thought he was mistaken. But about fifty days before the Assumption of the Blessed Virgin Mary during which all this happened to him, it was revealed to him that this was due to occur round about the time of the Assumption, but that prophecy he had forgotten. To the praise and glory of our Lord Jesus Christ. Amen.

Chapter 53

How the blessed Virgin appeared to Brother Conrad in the woods of Forano.

THE PROVINCE OF THE MARCHES OF ANCONA was distinguished by certain notable star-characters, namely holy friars minor, who above and here below in the near presence of God, shone with radiant virtues. Their memory is truly holy and blessed. Among them were some as it were major stars who outshone the others, namely Brother Lucidio the elder, shining with sanctity and burning with divine love, whose glorious tongue prompted by the Holy Spirit produced wonderful results. Likewise Brother Bentivoglia from San Severino who was seen uplifted a great distance into the air while he was praying in a wood, by Brother Masseo of the same locality who because of this miracle gave up his parish. He became a friar minor of such holy life that he accomplished many miracles and fell asleep at Morro. While the said Brother Bentivoglia was alone at Ponte della Trave caring for a leper, he was compelled in obedience to depart. Unwilling to abandon the leper he placed him on his shoulder and thus burdened made his way from Ponte della Trave to Mount San Vicino where there was another friary, covering a distance of fifteen miles. Carrying such a burden he could scarcely have flown the distance in such a short time even if he had been an eagle. All who heard of this divine miracle were filled with wonder and amazement.

Brother Peter of Monticello was seen by Brother Servadeo of Urbino, who was then warden of the ancient priory of Ancona, elevated to a lofty position up to the feet of Christ, some five or six cubits from the ground, that is, from the floor of the church. This brother having fasted most devoutly through the Lent of Saint Michael the archangel and shut himself in the church on the last day of his fast, was heard by a youthful friar who lay carefully hidden for the purpose beneath the altar, speaking with Saint Michael the archangel, and the archangel with him. And these were their words: said the archangel: "Brother Peter, you have labored faithfully on my behalf and done much penance, and humiliated yourself greatly; behold I have come to you that you may ask for any favor you wish and I will beg it from God for you." Brother Peter replied: "Most holy head of the heavenly court, most faithful upholder of the honor of God, most holy protector of souls, this is the favor I beg of you, that you obtain for me the remission of all my sins." The archangel replied: "Ask a different favor, for this one I can obtain for you very easily." But Brother Peter wanted nothing else. The archangel concluded by saying: "For your devotion and for the faith you have in me, the favor you request and many others I shall obtain for you." At the end of this colloquy which lasted a large part of the night, he left him inwardly comforted. At the same time the truly holy Brother Peter and the aforesaid Brother Conrad of Offida were also there. While they were in residence at the friary of Forano in the custody of Ancona, Brother Conrad went into the woods to meditate on divine things. Brother Peter stealthily followed him to see what would happen to him. Most devoutly and in tears Brother Conrad began to pray to the most blessed Virgin to obtain a favor for himself from her blessed Son, in order that he might be able to feel ever so slightly something of that beatitude felt by Saint Simon on that day of purification when he bore Christ the blessed Savior in his arms. His prayer was heard by that most blessed Lady, and behold there appeared the Queen of Glory along with her blessed Son in an intensity of light that not only dispersed the darkness but also outshone all other lights. As she drew near to Brother Conrad she placed in his arms that child who is more comely than all the sons of men. Brother Conrad taking him most devoutly, pressing his lip to lip and breast to breast, was wholly melted in embraces and kisses of love. Brother Peter beheld all these things in that bright light and derived wondrous comfort from them. When the blessed Virgin and her Son withdrew Brother Peter secretly remained behind in that blessed wood and then hurriedly returned to the friary. When Brother Conrad returned all elated and joyful, Brother Peter greeted him: "O celebate brother, a great consolation you have had this day." Said Brother Conrad: "What do you mean Brother Peter? How do you know what I have experienced?"

Brother Peter answered: "I am well aware, brother, that the most blessed Virgin and her Son visited you." When he heard this Brother Conrad as a truly humble man desiring secrecy, begged him to tell nobody. For there was such affection between these two men that they seemed to be as one heart and one soul.

At the friary of Sirolo Brother Conrad also freed a maiden possessed by a demon; he immediately fled from the friary lest the mother of the liberated maiden find him and there should be a concourse of people. For Brother Conrad had prayed all through that night and had appeared to the mother of the maiden; by thus appearing he had freed her daughter. To the praise and glory of our Lord Jesus Christ. Amen.

Chapter 54

How Christ appeared to Brother John of Alverna who in embracing Christ became rapt.

HOW GLORIOUS IS OUR FATHER FRANCIS in the sight of God appears in the chosen sons whom the Holy Spirit gathered in his Order; for the glory of so great a father lies in his understanding sons. Among them there shone especially the aforesaid Brother John, who in the skies of his Order sparkled like a wonderful star thanks to the splendor of his grace. For in his youth he had a heart matured by wisdom, and longed with all his might for the way of penance that ensures purity of body and mind. And so while he was still a little boy he would wear an iron belt next to his skin, and every day carried the cross of abstinence. Thus when he was with the canons at Saint Peter's at Fermo before he had taken the habit of the holy father, while they lived

128

lavishly, he disciplined himself with wonderfully strict abstinence.

But he had to suffer so many impediments to his angelic zeal from his companions: they deprived him of his breastplate and put obstacles in the way of his abstinence. Under God's inspiration he considered forsaking the world and those who loved it, and offering up the flower of his angelic youth to the arms of the Crucified within the order of the blessed Francis, in whom, as he had heard, the stigmata of Christ's crucifixion had been renewed. When therefore the youth had in the name of the Lord assumed the habit of the friars minor and was entrusted to a master for training in spiritual matters, he sometimes heard divine words from his master; then his heart would melt like wax; he was filled within with such grace of gentleness, that his outer self was sometimes constrained to run about the garden, sometimes through the church, sometimes right through the woods, running about in whatever way the fire within impelled him.

In the course of time God's grace raised up this angelic man by stages, sometimes to the splendor of the cherubim, sometimes to the ardor of the seraphim, sometimes to the joys of the angels. What is more, it sometimes drew him to the divine kisses and the overpowering embraces of the love of Christ, as of an intimate friend, not only because of his inner inclination, but also because of outward signs he showed. Thus it once happened to him that fired with the love of Christ, for the space of three years at least, he received wonderful consolations and so transformed was frequently rapt up to God. But because God takes special care of his sons, now consoling them with favors, now testing them with trials, while Brother John was in a certain friary, there was withdrawn from him that brightness and that fire; so he remained unloved, without light and in the greatest dejection. For this reason whenever his soul did not feel the presence of his beloved Master, he was distressed and tormented, anxiously bewailing a beloved one who with quiet restraint had concealed himself; but in no way and nowhere was he able to experience those sweet embraces and blessed kisses as he had been accustomed to do. This distress he endured for several days, mourning, sighing and weeping. But one day when he was walking through the aforementioned wood in which he had devised a path to walk on, and was walking along depressed and desolate, he leaned against a beech tree and raised a tear-stained face to heaven. And behold! He who heals the contrite in heart and lightens their afflictions, the blessed Lord Jesus Christ, appeared on the same path but said nothing. When Brother John recognized him, he immediately threw himself at his feet, and with uncontrollable groans begged him and most humbly besought him to come to his aid: "Without you, sweetest Savior, I remain in darkness and grief; without you, gentle lamb, I remain in perplexity and fear; without you, exalted Son of God, I remain in confusion and shame! Without you I am despoiled of all that is good; without you I am blinded with darkness, because you, Jesus, are the true light of the world. Without you I am lost and damned, for you are the life of souls and the life of lives. Without you I am sterile and arid, for you are the God of Gods who bestows favors. In you I find every consolation because you are God, our redemption, our love and our longing, the bread that restores us, the wine that gives joy to the choirs of angels and the hearts of all the saints. Enlighten me therefore, most gracious master and most kindly shepherd, for I am your lamb, however unworthy."

But because a desire deferred is kindled into a greater love, the blessed Christ withdrew along the path saying absolutely nothing to him. Then Brother

John, seeing that the blessed Christ was withdrawing without hearkening to his prayer, rose up again with a compelling and holy importunity like a needy pauper. Again he rushed forward towards Christ and prostrating himself humbly at his feet implored him more devoutly with tears: "O sweetest Jesus, have pity on my distress. Grant my prayer in the fulness of your mercy and in the truth of your salvation, and restore to me the joy of your salvation, for the earth is full of your mercy. You know how grievously I am distressed, I humbly beseech you to come to the aid of my darkened soul."

And again the Savior passed on without saying anything to Brother John, or giving him any consolation of any kind. He seemed intent on withdrawing along the aforesaid path the more to increase his clamoring, like a mother with a baby who has denied her child the breast when he has asked for it, and after it has cried, she hugs it and kisses it and takes it back all the more gently. And so Brother John following the blessed Christ for the third time, went his way weeping copiously like a baby seeking its mother, or a boy his father or a submissive pupil behind his compassionate teacher. When he had caught up with him, the blessed Christ turned his gracious face toward Brother John and spread out his venerable hands, like a priest when he turns toward the people. Then Brother John saw marvellous rays of light issuing forth from the most holy breast of Christ, not only lighting up the whole forest outwardly, but also inwardly filling body and soul with divine splendor. At once Brother John knew what humble and reverent act he should perform before the blessed Christ. He immediately threw himself at the feet of Christ. The blessed Christ in his compassion revealed to him those most holy feet over which Brother John shed so many tears that he seemed like another Mary Magdalen, begging him not to take account of his sins, but by his most sacred passion and the shedding of his precious blood, graciously to restore his soul to the favor of divine love.

"Since it is your commandment that I have the strength to love you with all my heart and with all my strength—a commandment that no man can fulfil without your aid—so help me, most loving Jesus Christ, that I may love you with all my strength."

While Brother John lay at Christ's feet praying fervently, he received so much grace from him that there and then he was fully restored, and like Mary Magdalen calmed and consoled. Then conscious of the gift of so much grace, Brother John began to render thanks to God and humbly to kiss Christ's feet, rising up in order to look upon the Savior while he thanked him. And the blessed Christ held forth and opened out his most holy hands to be kissed. And as he opened them Brother John arose and drawing near those hands embraced the Lord Jesus and the blessed Christ embraced him. Then as Brother John kissed the most holy breast of Christ, he became conscious of such a divine fragrance that if all the scents of the world were concentrated into one, it would be considered a putrid stench compared with that heavenly fragrance. And besides this there issued from the breast of the Savior the aforementioned rays of light illuminating his mind both within and without and everything round about. In the midst of this embrace, this fragrance, this illumination, on the very breast of Christ Brother John was rapt, completely comforted and wondrously enlightened. For henceforth having drunk from the sacred fountain of the Lord's breast, he was filled with the gift of wisdom and the grace of the Word of God, and frequently poured forth words that were wondrous beyond telling. And because there flowed forth from his belly rivers of living water that he had drunk from the depths of the bosom of the

Lord Jesus Christ, so did he transform the minds of those who heard him and produce wondrous fruits. Further, the aforesaid fragrance and splendor that he had sensed lasted in his soul for many days; and what is more, along the same path where the feet of the Lord had passed and for a wide distance around, he was for a long time conscious of the same light and fragrance.

As Brother John returned to himself after the aforesaid rapture the blessed Christ disappeared, but he thereafter remained consoled and illuminated. And thus he discovered the mercifulness of Christ, as the story was told to me by the one who had it from the mouth of Brother John. He discovered his soul buried in the depths of divine godliness, and this is confirmed by many obvious manifestations. For in the presence of the Roman curia, of kings and barons, and in the presence of teachers and learned doctors, he poured forth such sublime and profound enlightenment, that he moved them to wonder and amazement. Although Brother John was a virtually uneducated man yet he made amazing statements on most complicated and profound problems of the Trinity and many other mysteries of Scripture. For as is already clear, he was raised up first to the feet of Christ amid tears, then to Christ's hands with his arms, and thirdly to his blessed bosom, with rapture and rays of light. These are mighty mysteries that could not be explained in a few words. But he who wishes to know, let him read Bernard on the *Song of Songs,* who there sets forth these steps in order: the beginners to the feet, those already on the way to the hands, and the successful to the kissing and embracing. For the blessed Christ while saying nothing to Brother John, conferred such grace upon him, and demonstrated that like a good shepherd he was more concerned to nurture a human soul with heavenly feelings, than to make a big fuss for fleshly ears with exterior noises. For the kingdom of

God is not in outward but in inward things: "For all his glory cometh from within," says the prophet. To the praise of our Lord Jesus Christ.

Chapter 55

How a heavenly answer was given to Brother John of Alverna praying on behalf of a certain brother.

BROTHER JOHN WAS REQUESTED by Brother James of Fallerone to intercede with God for some scruple of conscience that was greatly worrying him, namely concerning certain matters pertaining to his priestly office. He received an answer before the feast of Saint Lawrence, as the Lord told it to him. He relates that the Lord said to him: "He is a priest according to God's ordinance." But when John's conscience still pricked him he again begged James to ask God's will in the matter.

As he faithfully kept the vigil of Saint Lawrence by night, watching and praying to the Lord to reassure him by the merits of Saint Lawrence concerning his scruples of conscience, there appeared to him as he watched and prayed the blessed Lawrence clad in a white raiment like a Levite, and said to him: "I am the Levite Lawrence. He for whom you are praying is a priest according to God's ordinance." And so he was reassured and greatly consoled for the doubt he had felt.

On another occasion there appeared to the same Brother John while the friars were singing *Salve regina* one evening, Saint Lawrence in the form of a youth, clad in a red dalmatic and bearing a gridiron. "This little gridiron," he said, "brought me heavenly glory, and the pain of the burning coals revealed to me the fulness of the mercy of God." And he added: "If you wish to earn the glory and mercy of God, endure uncomplainingly the bitterness of this world." Saint Lawrence remained with him thus visible until the singing of the antiphon came to an end. The friars then went off for a spell but he remained in the choir with Saint Lawrence. Having reassured Brother John he then disappeared leaving him filled with such love and affection that for the whole night of the said feast he did not sleep but spent it all in wonderful relief.

The same Brother John was once celebrating mass very devoutly. While the Host was being consecrated, the form of the bread was transformed before his very eyes, and in an instant Christ appeared to him clad in a red robe and gave him such gentle comfort that if it had not been for his lingering consciousness he would have been caught up in ecstasy. And in the same vision he was assured that thanks to that mass the Lord was placated for the whole world and especially for those souls entrusted to his care. To the praise and glory of our Lord Jesus Christ.

Chapter 56

How Brother John while celebrating mass saw souls being released from Purgatory.

WHILE THE SAID BROTHER JOHN was celebrating

mass for the souls of the dead, he offered up that loftiest of all sacraments with such outpouring of love and compassion—the efficacy of which is desired by the souls of the dead above all else—that he seemed completely melted in the earnestness of his devotion and honey-sweet love coming from above. When therefore during that holy mass he reverently raised up the most sacred body of the Lord, offering it to God the Father in order that through the love of him who hung upon the Cross he might liberate souls created by him and mercifully free them from Purgatory, he beheld almost countless souls issue forth from Purgatory, like a multitude of sparks issuing from a blazing furnace. And he saw them flying up to their heavenly home through the merits of Christ who hung on the Cross for the salvation of mankind, and who is offered up daily in the most sacred Host for the living and the dead; he, that blessed God, who is man, life and Redeemer, justice and everlasting sanctification, for ever and ever.

Chapter 57

How Brother John saw the blessed Francis with many brothers and how Brother John spoke to him after his death.

AT THE TIME WHEN BROTHER JAMES OF FALLERONE, a holy man, lay ill at the friary of Mogliano in the custody of Fermo and the provinces of the Marches, Brother John of Alverna prayed to God for Brother

James in fervent mental prayer and with heartfelt sincerity, for he loved him dearly as if he were his own father. And while he prayed thus fervently he fell into an ecstasy and saw a host of many angels and saints hovering in the air in brilliant light over his cell, which was in the woods. So intense was the light that all the countryside glowed. Among the angels he saw the stricken Brother James for whom he was praying standing there resplendent in white clothes. There too he saw our blessed Father Francis marked with the sacred stigmata and resplendent in wondrous glory. He saw and recognized the saintly Brother Lucidio and the aged Brother Matthew of Monte Rubbiano; and several other friars he recognized whom he had never seen in this life, who together with a host of saints shone in glory.

And while Brother John gazed on these things there came to him an assuring revelation concerning the salvation of the sufferer, that as a result of his illness he was destined to pass over to God; but he was not to go to heaven immediately because he must be purified for a short space. Brother John who witnessed all this rejoiced so much over the salvation and glory of the aforementioned friar, that he frequently addressed Brother James with spiritual compassion, saying in the secret places of his heart: "Brother James, my brother, most faithful servant of Christ; Brother James, sweetest father; Brother James, companion of the angels and of the blessed saints." Being sure of the death of Brother James and rejoicing at the salvation of his soul, he departed from the friary of Massa where he had had this vision and went to visit Brother James at Mogliano, where he found the sick man so laid low with suffering that he could scarcely speak. To him Brother John announced that he was going to die and like a carefree joyous lion was passing over to eternal life.

Brother James, himself now completely confident

of his salvation, welcomed him with a beautiful smile and joyful face because he had brought him such joyful news. And because Brother James loved him like a son, he commended himself to Brother John and let him know that his soul was now being released from his body. Brother John asked him to do him the favor of speaking to him after his death, which Brother James promised provided the kindness of the Savior permitted it. And after these words as the hour of death was approaching Brother James began to repeat devoutly: "In peace, may I both sleep and rest." And with these words, with joyful and serene countenance he passed on to the Lord Jesus Christ. Brother John, having returned to the friary of Massa, awaited the fulfilment of Brother James's promise to speak to him on the day he said he would. As he waited, there appeared to him Christ in a great light with a wondrous company of angels and saints. Brother John remembered Brother James and commended him to Christ. Next day while Brother John was in the woods of Massa Brother James appeared to him, all glorious and rejoicing accompanied by angels. Said Brother John: "O father, why did you not speak to me on the day you promised?" he replied: "Because I was in some slight need of purification. But at that same hour that Christ appeared to you, I appeared to holy lay-brother James of Massa, while he was still alive and serving mass. And there he beheld the sacred Host at the moment of the elevation transformed into a very handsome youth. And I spoke to the brother thus: 'This day with that youth I go forward to the kingdom, because without him nobody can go there.' And when you commended me to Christ, your prayer was answered. In the same hour when I spoke to Brother James I was liberated." And with these words he went on his way to the Lord. Brother John remained greatly consoled; but Brother James of Fallerone went on his way on the Vigil of Saint Paul in the month of July and now rests in the friary of Mogliano where he performs many miracles. To the praise of God.

Chapter 58

How Brother John acquired the spirit of revelation.

CERTAIN PERSONS WERE POSSESSED of certain terrible sins that no man could know about except by divine revelation. Some of them died, others were still alive. To those still living Brother John disclosed their secret sins by divine revelation. These were thereby converted to a life of penance. One of them said that the sin Brother John had revealed he had committed before Brother John was born into this world. I was told this by the man to whom he spoke. And they confessed that what Brother John said about them was the truth. It was revealed to the same man that some who were dead died a temporal and eternal death, others only a temporal death; and this was demonstrated to him beyond all doubt. And I saw the trustworthy friar who knew these persons.

Chapter 59

The vision of Brother Leo and how the same vision was revealed to Saint Francis.

AT ONE TIME WHEN SAINT FRANCIS was grievously ill Brother Leo tended him with great devotion and care. On one occasion when Brother Leo was at the side of the blessed Francis and was engaged in prayer, he fell into a trance and was taken to a certain very big fast-flowing river, fast-flowing and wide. Here as he watched those crossing he saw some friars walking into the river bearing burdens. They were immediately toppled over by the violence of the river and swallowed up in the devouring depths. Some got as far as a third of the way across and drowned, others half-way, yet others nearly all the way. All of them thanks to the baggage or loads they carried were drowned and died a cruel and relentless death in various ways differing according to their loads. Brother Leo, seeing such danger, felt pity for them. And behold! there suddenly appeared a few brothers without any burden or pack of any kind. Their only guiding light was their poverty. They stepped into the river and crossed over unharmed.

Saint Francis divined in the spirit that Brother Leo had seen some vision and when he had returned to himself called him and said: "Tell me, what did you see?" And he duly recounted everything he had seen. Then said Francis: "What you saw was real, for the river is this world. The brothers who are swallowed up by the river are those who do not follow out their evangelical profession and vows of voluntary poverty.

Those who crossed unharmed are the brothers who possessed the spirit of God, who neither seek or possess anything earthly or anything carnal, but 'having food and raiment are content' (I Timothy 6:8). They follow the example of the naked crucified Christ, embrace every day the burden of his Cross, his light and acceptable yoke of obedience. Thus without difficulty or danger they pass over from the things of this world to eternity." To the praise of our Lord Jesus Christ.

Chapter 60

How a certain mighty tyrant seeing one of the companions of Saint Francis elevated three times to the top of his palace was converted to the Lord and became a friar minor.

THIS WAS A VERY OBVIOUS SIGN that the Order of the blessed Francis was founded by God: that as soon as it began to increase it began to spread almost to the ends of the earth. Saint Francis therefore, eager to conform to Christ in all things, used to send his friars two by two to preach throughout all countries. And such wondrous things the Lord accomplished through them that "their voice goes out through all the earth, and their words to the end of the world" (Psalm 19 [18]:4). Once it so fell out that two of those inexperienced disciples of the true father, travelling into unknown parts, reached a certain stronghold full of extremely wicked men. In it there was also a certain great tyrant, very cruel and impious, the head and leader of those robbers and evil men. He was of noble stock but of evil and despicable character. When these two friars meekly reached this castle in the evening, worn out with hunger, cold and fatigue—like lambs among wolves—they begged this lordly tyrant through a messenger to grant them hospitality overnight for the love of our Lord Jesus Christ. Inspired by the Lord he gladly welcomed them and showed them much compassion and courtesy. He had a big fire lit for them and a meal prepared for them in lordly style. While the brothers and all the other occupants were relaxing, one of the brothers who was a priest possessing a unique gift of speaking about God, noticed that none of those resting discussed or talked about God or the salvation of the soul, but only about robberies, murders and many other misdeeds that they had committed at various times, and that they gloried in the evil deeds and wickednesses they had committed everywhere. This friar therefore, refreshed in body and desiring to refresh his host and the others with heavenly food, said to the master: "My lord, you have shown us great courtesy and kindness; we would therefore be very ungrateful if we did not take pains to repay you with good things according to the will of God. We therefore beg you to assemble your whole household that we may make spiritual repayment for the physical favors we received from you." The lord of the house agreed to their request and caused everybody to assemble in the presence of the friars.

So the friar began to speak about the glory of paradise: "For there is eternal bliss, there the company of angels, the security of the blessed, there infinite glory; there abundance of heavenly treasures; there life everlasting, light unspeakable, untroubled peace, health incorruptible; there the presence of God—all that is good and nothing evil. And man because of his sins and abjectness, squanders so many good things and goes to hell, where there is pain and everlasting gloom, the company of devils, serpents and dragons, where there is untold misery, and life without life, tangible darkness and the presence of Lucifer; where there is confusion and wrath, everlasting fire and ice, worms and fury, hunger and thirst, death without death, groanings, tears, gnashing of teeth and an eternity of torment; where there is everything evil and an absence of anything good! And all of you, as I have perceived, are running headlong into such evils, for in you there appears nothing in the way of good deeds or words. Wherefore I counsel and admonish you, dear friends, do not cast away those lofty heavenly blessings that will endure for eternity for the worthless things of this world and the possessions of the flesh that all pass away like a shadow; do not hasten on your way to such fearful and horrible torments."

At these words uttered by the friar at the prompting of the Holy Spirit, the lord of the castle was touched within; his heart stung with remorse, he fell down at the friar's feet. Together with all present he began to weep most bitterly, begging and praying him to guide them to the way of salvation. When he had made his confession with many tears and sincere remorse, the friar told him that for the expiation of his sins he must make pilgrimages to shrines, suffer the pangs of fasting, watch and pray, and persevere with generous alms-giving and other good works.

The lord replied: "Dear father, I have never been out of this province. I do not know how to say *Our Father, Hail Mary* or any other prayers. So please impose on me some other penance." Then the holy frair said: "Beloved, I am willing to go surety on your behalf, and thanks to God's goodness to make intercession to the Lord Jesus Christ for your sins that your soul may not perish. Now for the present, I want you to do no other penance than to bring me tonight with your own hands some straw for my companion and myself to sleep on."

Joyfully he brought the straw and carefully prepared

143

a bed in a room where a light was shining. The lord of the castle on the evidence of the holy and virtuous words the friar had uttered, realized that he was a saintly man, and set his heart on observing what he would do that night. And he observed that at a late hour the holy brother lay down in bed to sleep. When he thought everybody was sound asleep, he arose in the silence of the night, stretched out his hands to the Lord and prayed for him for whom he stood surety and for the forgiveness of his sins. And behold! even as he prayed he was elevated into the air up to the roof-top of the castle, and up there in the air wept and grieved so much for the soul of the lord, begging for his forgiveness, that there has scarcely ever been seen a man who wept so sorely for beloved kinsmen or departed friends as did this friar for that man's sins. That night he was thrice lifted up in the air amid pious lamentations and tears of compassion, and the lord of the castle witnessing all these events unobserved, could hear his affectionate grieving and sighs and behold his tears of compassion. Rising early in the morning he fell at the friar's feet and with tears of remorse begged him to set him on the path of salvation, resolutely prepared for any command he might give. At the suggestion of the holy friar therefore he sold all his possessions, made restitution of what had to be restored, and all the rest he distributed to the poor as the Gospel bids us; offering himself to God he entered the order of the friars minor and with praiseworthy steadfastness ended his days in sanctity.

His followers and other companions, their hearts smitten with remorse, changed their lives for the better. Thus did the holy simplicity of those friars bear fruit: they preached not about Aristotle and the philosophers, but about the pains of hell and the glory of paradise with the economy of words prescribed in the Holy Rule. To the praise of our Lord Jesus Christ who is blessed for ever. Amen.

Chapter 61

Blessed Francis's dislike of study.

A CERTAIN FRIAR MINOR, namely John of Sciaca, in the days of blessed Francis was a priest at Bologna—a very cultured man. Without permission from the blessed Francis he instituted a course of study at Bologna. It was reported to blessed Francis while he was absent, that such a course had been instituted at Bologna. He immediately went to Bologna and severely reprimanded the priest saying: "You want to destroy my Order: I desired and wished, following the example of my Lord Jesus Christ, that my brethren should pray rather than read." Leaving Bologna Saint Francis pronounced a grievous curse upon him. After the pronouncement of the curse the friar began to fail in health. Grievously ill he sent a request through the brothers asking Saint Francis to lift the curse. Blessed Francis replied: "The curse with which I cursed him was confirmed in heaven by the blessed Lord Jesus Christ; he remains accursed." So the afflicted minister lay on his bed dejected and without consolation.

And behold there descended from the heights of heaven a drop of sulphurous fire upon his body, passing through him and the bed on which he lay, and amid the foulest stench the unhappy man expired and the Devil took his soul.

Chapter 62

How blessed Francis forbade the brethren to retain property for holy purposes.

PETER OF CATANIA, a vicar of Saint Francis, once observed a throng of friars from other institutions crowding into Saint Mary's of Porziuncula, which was not well equipped for providing for the necessities of life. He said to Saint Francis: "Father, with so many friars flocking in from everywhere I do not know what to do. I have not the means to cope adequately. I beg you that it be your pleasure to set aside some of the goods of the recent novices. Let the question of how they are spent be reviewed at a later time." Saint Francis replied: "Away with that sort of piety, beloved brother, that would permit of unworthy action within the Rule for the sake of any man!" He: "What then am I to do?" Saint Francis: "Strip the altar of the Virgin and remove the various ornaments, since otherwise you will be unable to come to the aid of the needy. Believe me, the Mother of God would rather have the Gospel of her Son observed and her altar stripped, than have an altar adorned and her Son outraged. The Lord will send someone to restore to his Mother what she has lent to us."

At times too the saint used to reiterate these words: "As far as the brethren turn aside from poverty, so far will the world turn aside from them." And he said, "They will seek and not find. But if they embrace my Lady Poverty the world will nourish them because they are given to the world for its salvation."

The blessed Francis would often say to the friars: "These three things I commend to you, namely: restraint in the face of an unbridled appetite for knowledge; prayer, which the Devil with many futile efforts is ever intent on nullifying; and the love of poverty, and holy poverty itself."

Chapter 63

Three things that displeased Christ in the friars of the blessed Francis.

ON ONE OCCASION CHRIST said to Brother Leo, a companion of the blessed Francis: "I am grieved concerning the brethren." Brother Leo replied: "How so?" He said: "For three reasons, namely, because they do not appreciate the benefit I have bestowed on them, as you well know; every day I give abundantly while they neither sow nor reap; and also because all day they grumble and are idle, and because they often provoke one another to anger and do not return to their affection or forgive the offences they receive." Once at Saint Mary's of Porziuncula the blessed Francis, pondering how much benefit of prayer was lost through idle words, uttered after prayer, ordained this remedy against the uttering of idle words saying: "Whosoever utters an idle word, let him be obliged to confess his guilt and for each idle word to say a *Pater noster*. This is my wish; if he has already condemned himself for a sin committed, let him say a *Pater noster* for his own soul; if he has already been reproved by another let him direct the prayer to the soul of him who reproved him."

Chapter 64

The vision of a judgment seen by Brother Leo.

THIS WAS BROTHER LEO'S VISION: he saw in his dreams the preparation for the Last Judgment. Angels were blowing their trumpets and a multitude was gathering in a vast field. And behold! two ladders had been placed in position one on each side. One was red the other white; both reached from earth to heaven.

At the top of the red ladder appeared Christ as if angry and aggrieved, and blessed Francis near him but lower down. Descending a little way he kept calling out: "Come brothers, come! Climb up to the Lord who is calling you! Have courage! Be not afraid, come!" Many brothers were gathering for the Judgment. Trusting in the call of Saint Francis they ran and began to ascend the red ladder energetically. As they climbed up one would fall from the third step, another from the fourth, another from the tenth, others from half-way, and others from near the top.

Blessed Francis beholding this and moved with compassion at such a fall, appealed to Christ as Judge on behalf of his sons. Christ showed blessed Francis his hands and side where the reopened wounds were visible from which the blood dropped freely. And he kept repeating: "Behold what your friars have done to me," while blessed Francis continued to beg mercy for the brethren. After a brief respite he came down a few more steps and said: "Do not despair but have confidence! Hasten to the white ladder! Hasten and climb up! There you will be welcomed! By it you will enter heaven!" The friars rushed towards the white ladder at the father's prompting, and behold! the Virgin Mary Mother of Christ appeared at the top of the ladder and received them and they entered the kingdom of heaven without difficulty.

Chapter 65

Tribulation in the Order.

HOLY BROTHER CONRAD has related—as he had the story from Brother Leo—that Saint Francis was once praying at Saint Mary of the Angels behind the pulpit of the church. He held his hands outstretched to heaven saying: "O Lord, have pity on your people, spare them!" Christ appeared to him saying: "Your prayer is a good one and I grant it willingly, because the cost to me is great and I have paid a great price. Nevertheless do one thing for me and I shall have mercy on all the people, that your Order may continue to exist and be mine exclusively. But the time will come when it will turn away from me; but I shall continue to uphold the Order for the world's sake, because it has confidence in the Order as its light and guide. But hereafter I shall confer power on demons who will stir up many scandals and troubles for them everywhere so that they will be expelled and shunned by everybody. And if a son goes to his father's house, instead of bread he will give him a blow on the head with a staff. And if the brothers knew of the troubles of those days they would begin to scatter, and many will flee to desert places." And blessed Francis asked the Lord: "Lord, how will they exist there?" Christ answered: "I who fed the sons of Israel in the desert shall feed them there with herbs and shall give those herbs various tastes, such as that of manna; and thereafter these men will go and reconstruct the Order in its original and perfect state. For woe unto those who are self-satisfied with the mere appearances of conversation, who grow slack and slothful and constantly yield to temptations permitted for the testing of the elect; for only those who have been tested and meanwhile suffer from the malice of the wicked shall receive the crown of life. To the praise of our Lord Jesus Christ. Praise to God the Father . . ."

Chapter 66

The constancy of a soldier who entered the Order of Minors.

THERE WAS A CERTAIN VALIANT SOLDIER who won many victories and later became a friar minor. When soldiers laughed at him for entering such an Order when he could have joined the Templars or some such Order where he could do much good and remain in military service, he replied: "I tell you, when I am thirsty, hungry, cold and so on, I am at the same time assailed by suggestions of pride, concupiscence and so on. How much worse would it be if I saw my feet shod with iron and rode a handsome horse and so on." And he added: "Up to now I have been brave in attacking others; henceforth I wish to be brave in attacking myself." Thanks be to God.

Here ends the book of certain wonderful acts of the blessed Saint Francis and of his earliest companions.

Chapter 67

Concerning a noble friar who refused to go begging and thanks to his merit in sacred obedience, humility and obedience lost his sense of shyness.

IN NEW BURGUNDY there was a certain young friar named Michael of noble family, who out of a sense of shame refused absolutely to go out begging. It so fell out that blessed Francis came that way and was informed of the accusation against the friar. He reprimanded him very severely and ordered him in holy obedience to go alone and naked except for a loincloth to a certain castle about a mile away to beg for alms.

In humble obedience he went off scantily clad, and setting aside all sense of shyness. Bread he received in plenty, also grain and other things, returning home laden. And from then on he experienced such joy and grace that he never wanted to do anything else but go begging.

Chapter 68

How the blessed Virgin appeared to a certain brother sick unto death.

IN THE MARCHES there was a certain friar of such admirable sanctity and grace that he seemed wholly godlike. Sometimes when he was rapt and raised up to God there came birds of divers kinds and settled very tamely on his head, hands and arms and there sang wonderfully. He always remained alone, spoke very rarely and neither by day nor by night ceased from prayer and divine contemplation. Having lived his life out commendably and virtuously he came to his end. And when he was sick unto death and would eat nothing, he was miraculously visited and consoled by the most blessed Virgin Mary, Queen of Mercy.

One day there appeared to him the most blessed and glorious Mother of Christ with a great throng of angels and holy virgins. When he beheld her, greatly uplifted and consoled, he begged urgently to be led forth from the dark prison of the flesh. The blessed Virgin replied: "Fear not, my son, your request will be granted."

Together with the most blessed Mother of Christ there were three virgins, each of them bearing a box with an electuary of wondrous fragrance and indescribable sweetness. And the most blessed Mother taking one of the boxes gave to the sick brother a little of the heavenly electuary. When he had tasted it he experienced such beatitude, that it seemed as if his soul would leave his body. To the blessed Virgin he said: "No more, O most blessed and sweet Lady, for I cannot bear such sweetness." But the most holy and merciful Mother encouraged him in the hope of life eternal, and continually offering the electuary to him emptied the whole of the first box. When the blessed Virgin took up the second box the patient said: "O most blessed Mother, if my soul is almost melted at the fragrance and sweetness of the first electuary, how shall I be able to bear the second? I beg you, O blessed above all others, not to offer me more." But the very blessed Virgin said: "Son, taste a little of this second electuary." And when she had given him a little she said: "Take henceforth what can suffice for you, but be strengthened, my son, because I shall soon return to you and to the kingdom of my Son for which you have so ardently longed, and into which you have ever prayed that I should introduce you." Bidding him farewell she vanished from his sight. But he remained in such spiritual bliss that for several days he lived on without bodily nourishment, miraculously sustained and satisfied. And on the last day of his life in the company of the brethren and speaking to them with great serenity of mind and body, he passed over to the Lord in exaltation.

Chapter 69

How an angel of the Lord spoke to Brother John of Penna while he was still a boy in secular dress.

BROTHER JOHN OF PENNA was still a boy in secular dress when one night there appeared to him a very handsome youth who said: "John, go to San Stefano, for there one of my friars will be preaching; have confidence in his teaching and attend to his words, for I have sent him. You have a long journey to make and afterwards you will come to me."

He immediately arose and was conscious of a wonderful change in his soul. Going to the place mentioned he found Brother Philip proclaiming the kingdom of God, not in learned words of human wisdom, but by virtue of the Holy Spirit. When the sermon was over Brother John went to the preacher and said: "Father, if it were your pleasure to receive me into the Order I would willingly do penance and serve the Lord Jesus Christ."

The holy and enlightened friar perceiving in the youth wondrous innocence and willingness said to him: "See to it that you come to me on a certain day in the city of Recanati and I shall have you admitted." The youth pondered in his heart saying: "This will be the long journey I am to make, and afterwards go to heaven as was revealed to me." He went therefore, was immediately received into the Order and expected to go on to his God. But in the chapter the minister said: "If anyone wishes to go to the province of Provence by merit of holy obedience, I shall send him." When Brother John heard this he made ready to go thither, thinking in his heart that this probably was the long journey he was to make. Confiding in Brother Philip who had had him admitted, he asked him to obtain for him this favor that he might go to the province of Provence to dwell there; for in those days friars hoped to go to foreign provinces in order to be "pilgrims and strangers" in this world, and citizens and servants of God in heaven. Brother Philip, seeing the sincerity and holiness of his intention, obtained for him permission to go to the said province. Brother John believed that this journey accomplished would lead him on to heaven.

He remained in the province for thirty years, living an exemplary life of the greatest sanctity and hoping every day for the fulfilment of the promise. Although he grew in purity of life and extreme sanctity, was uniquely beloved throughout the entire province, both by friars and laity, yet he could see no sign that his desire was being in any way fulfilled. One day when he was praying and lamenting before God that his living on earth was being excessively prolonged, behold! Jesus Christ appeared to him. At the sight of Christ his soul was melted. The Lord Jesus Christ said to him: "Son, ask from me whatever you wish." He replied: "Lord, I desire nothing but yourself; but this one thing I beg, that you pardon my sins and grant me the grace to see you again when my need is greater." And the Lord said: "Your prayer is granted" and disappeared from his sight. He remained wholly comforted by the Lord.

At last the friars in the Marches arranged with the general that the brother should return to the Marches. When Brother Philip saw it as a matter of obedience he pondered in his heart saying: "This is the long journey by which you shall come to God." Having returned to the Marches he waited from day to day for the fulfilment of the promise made to him. But the journey was further prolonged, for he lived for a good thirty years after his return to the Marches. He became a warden many times over. Through him the Lord worked many miracles and he acquired the spirit of prophecy. On one occasion when he was absent from his friary, one of his novices was tempted by the Devil to abandon the Order. He made a pact with temptation and tempter that when Brother John returned, he himself would immediately leave. As soon as Brother John returned he at once summoned the young man and said: "Come, my son, I want you to confess. But first listen to me, my son." And then he told the novice the full story of his temptation, then added: "Because you waited and did not wish to withdraw without my blessing, God will grant the favor that you will never leave this Order, but with God's blessing will die in it." Whereupon the novice was confirmed in his good intention and was made a holy friar. This whole story was told to me, Brother Ugolino, by Brother John himself.

Brother John was always a man of a quiet disposition, subdued, who rarely spoke; a man of great devoutness, constant in prayer. It was his special habit after matins not to return to his cell. Once after matins, as he was praying fervently, an angel of the Lord appeared to him and said: "Brother John, completed is the journey, as you have so long expected. So I announce to you on God's behalf, that you choose whatever favor you desire, and that in addition you choose for yourself either one whole day in Purgatory or seven days of suffering in this world." When Brother John had chosen seven days of suffering in this world, he was suddenly stricken with a succession of infirmities. He was plagued now with noisomeness, now with pains, now with gout, now with convulsions, now with pains in the intestines and many other frailties. But what was worse than all the other afflictions was that a certain evil spirit would stand before him holding a mighty scroll recording all his sins, misdeeds and shortcomings. And the Devil would say to him: "Because of all these things that you have thought, said and done, you are damned." The suffering friar forgot all the good he had ever done, could not remember that he was in orders, or ever had been. He now considered himself completely damned as the evil spirit kept telling him. And so whenever he was asked by anybody how he was feeling he would reply: "Badly, because I am damned."

The friars sent for Brother Matthew of Monte Rubiano, a holy man who dearly loved Brother John. He came to him on the seventh day of his affliction and greeted him saying: "How is it, beloved brother?" The reply was: "Badly, because I am damned." Brother Matthew: "How can you say that? Do you not remember that you have often confessed to me, and that I gave you complete absolution? that you have

156

served God for many years in this holy Order, that heavenly mercy transcends all the sins of the world and Christ the Savior paid an infinite price on our behalf? So be steadfast and confident that you will be saved and not damned." Then because the term of seven days was completed, his temptation departed, and blessing came upon him with great joy. He told Brother Matthew he was going to his rest. After this the Lord Jesus Christ again appeared to him in great splendor and sweet fragrance, as he had promised him that he would appear at the right time. And he, full of joy, assured, consoled, with hands clasped and rendering thanks departed from the body and passed over to Christ the Lord, to whom be the praise, the honor and the glory. Amen.

Chapter 70

The vision of a certain brother in which he saw friars minor being damned.

THIS IS THE STORY of a certain friar who had visited the province of England. He had heard from a minister of that province, a man of great piety and sanctity, that a certain friar accustomed to experiences of ecstasy, had remained for a whole day in one continuous rapture drenched in tears. When the minister witnessed this he said: "This friar is dying," and he said to him: "O brother, I command you under your obedience to come out of your rapture." The friar at once came to himself and asked for food. When he had eaten the minister said: "I command you under obedience, to tell me the cause of your weeping, as we have never seen this happen to you before. It seems to be rather contrary to the nature of a rapture." As the friar could not remain silent but in fact had to confess, he said that he saw the Lord Jesus Christ on his lofty throne surrounded by the heavenly host ready to pronounce judgment; and when he had seen not only laymen but also clerics and adherents of different religions being condemned, he finally saw being brought in a certain man in the habit of a friar minor, very elegantly clad in a very costly habit. When questioned about his status or condition this man testified that he was a friar minor. Then said the judge: "Brother Francis, you hear what this man says. What do you say?" "Away with him, Lord," replied Francis, "for my friars are clad in humble clothes not costly ones." And immediately the unhappy man was cast into hell by demons.

And behold! another impressive man was brought in accompanied by several laymen. When questioned he said he was a friar minor. Again the Lord addressed the blessed Francis as before. In reply he said: "Lord, my friars follow a course of prayer and spiritual progress, and shun the affairs of worldly men." He suffered the same fate. And behold! there came another, laden with mighty packs of sumptuous and useless books. He was dealt with in the same way as the first and second. And behold! yet another, pre-occupied and absorbed with planning extensive and excessively luxurious buildings. Him too Francis refused to acknowledge as belonging to his Order. Finally there came one man, very lowly both in habit and appearance. When questioned who he was, he confessed he was a great sinner unworthy of any good thing, and begged for mercy. Embracing him Francis led him into glory with him, saying, "Lord, this man is a true friar minor."—"And that," said the friar to his minister, "was the reason for my weeping."

Chapter 71

How the blessed Jesus Christ, on the supplication of Saint Francis, caused a rich and courteous knight who had shown him great respect, to be converted and become a friar.

NOTE: THE EDITOR OR THE "ACTUS" confesses that he has been unable to discover the original text of this chapter, referred to in the numbering but absent in the Latin texts. It appears that all that has survived is the chapter heading.

Chapter 72

How the case of Brother Elias was revealed to blessed Francis, and of the efficacy of the prayer of blessed Father Francis on behalf of Elias in obtaining pardon from God.

THE MOST BLESSED FATHER FRANCIS by his fervent prayers reversed the sweeping sentence of God against a sinner, as is clear from the case of Brother Elias, who was second General Minister after blessed Francis. The apostasy of Brother Elias from the Order and from the Church, and his damnation, were revealed to the blessed Francis by the Lord. For this reason blessed Francis shunned Brother Elias to the extent that he would not walk along the same path as Brother Elias, look at him, speak with him, consort with him or eat with him. Noticing this, Brother Elias asked blessed Francis why he thus avoided him. In reply blessed Francis told him it was because he was damned and destined to apostasy. On hearing this Brother Elias burst into tears, and prostrating himself at his feet said: "I beseech you to entreat God on my behalf, a lamb of your flock, for I have such faith in your prayers that if I were in the depths of hell and you entreated God on my behalf, I should feel some relief, all the more so as God knows how to modify his judgment if a man forsakes evildoing. Intercede therefore with God on my behalf."

Blessed father Francis, moved by the tears of Brother Elias, betook himself to pray for him, and his prayer was answered by the Lord himself. He told Brother Elias that he would not be damned but that he would apostatize. And so it fell out, for Brother Elias was removed from his office as general by Pope Gregory IX. In his stead there was chosen his brother Albert of Pisa, then minister of England. Elias became a supporter of the Emperor Frederick. For this reason he was excommunicated by the Pope and deprived of the habit of the Order. While Brother Elias was in Sicily and in failing health, his blood brother, who was a friar minor and a lay brother, obtained permission and went to Sicily to visit him. Finding him ill he succeeded in getting Brother Elias to repent by admitting his guilt and to write a letter to the Pope.

This letter his brother conveyed to the Pope and from him obtained a dispensation to be absolved and invested with the habit of the Order. He returned to his brother who was still alive. And so Brother Elias was absolved from excommunication and reinvested with the habit of the Order. Administering the sacraments of the Church he ended his life in peace, saved by the prayers and merits of blessed Francis.

Chapter 73

How the venerable Brother Simon delivered from great temptation a certain brother who because of it proposed to give up the habit.

IN THE EARLIEST DAYS of the Order when Saint Francis was still alive, there came to the Order a certain young man called Brother Simon of Assisi, whom the All-Highest had endowed with such grace of blessedness and gentleness, and had raised to such holiness of mind and contemplation, that his whole life was a mirror of holiness and in his soul could be seen the reflection of divine kindliness. As I have heard from those who had association with him, he was very rarely seen outside his cell; when in the company of friars he busied himself with communicating with God. He never even learned Latin and almost always stayed in the woods. Yet he uttered such eminently lofty thoughts about God and the love of Christ, that his words seemed more than human. One evening when he had gone into the woods with Brother James of Massa and others to talk about God, he spoke so gently and devoutly about the love of Christ, as I was told by one who was present, that though they spent the whole night thus talking, it seemed to them that they had been there a very short time.

Brother Simon enjoyed such tranquillity of spirit that when he sensed the coming of divine visitations and outbursts of love, he would go to bed as if to sleep, because the quiet gentleness of the Holy Spirit called not only for peace of mind, but also of the body. Hence he was often enraptured during such visitations and became insensitive to outward things.

It happened on one occasion when he was drawn to heavenly things and inwardly on fire with divine favors and outwardly seemed quite insensitive, that a certain friar wishing to ascertain by experiment whether he was as insensitive as he seemed, placed a burning coal on his foot; it remained there until it went out. But Brother Simon felt nothing, and what was more miraculous, he suffered no bodily hurt from the fire.

Once when he was fervently talking to the friars about God a certain very ostentatious young man was converted to the Lord. In worldly life he had been licentious, of noble rank and addicted to pleasure. Brother Simon gave him a religious habit, and kept his civilian clothes. But the Devil who can breathe flame into live coals, so inflamed carnal desires in the young man, that despairing of being able to resist such temptation, he went frequently to Brother Simon saying: "Give me back the worldly clothes that I had, for I cannot endure so many temptations." Brother Simon taking pity on him began to talk to him about God, and very impressively and immediately extinguished the flames of desire. Tortured by a final and more serious temptation and repeating the words about his clothes, he decided firmly to return to worldly life, saying he was unable to endure such burning desires. Then Brother Simon, taking pity on him said: "Come my son, and sit beside me." In deep distress, sitting next to the father, he devoutly reclined his head on his bosom. Brother Simon, raising his eyes to heaven prayed for him so fervently that he was enraptured and his prayer was finally heard. Thus the young man was completely released from temptation, so that the ardour of desire was converted into the ardour of great love.

One day when a certain evil-doer had been condemned to lose his eyes, this young man, prompted by great fervor and gentle holiness, went to the rector and in the presence of his council begged him for the love of God to revoke such a serious sentence. When the rector contemptuously rejected his plea, the young man even more seriously impassioned, more humbly and in tears begged that his own eyes be gouged out to expiate the crime of the evil-doer, whose eyes should be spared, since he probably lacked the necessary fortitude. The rector in admiration for the young man's charity pardoned the evil-doer completely.

At one time when Brother Simon was in the forest of Brufort giving his time to prayer, he was disturbed by a multitude of chattering birds of some kind. He bade them in the name of the Lord to depart thence and not on any account to return. At his bidding in fact the birds withdrew and thereafter did not return thither.

Chapter 74

How the blessed Virgin Mother of our Lord and Saint John the Evangelist appeared to Brother Peter of Montecchio.

BROTHER PETER OF MONTECCHIO WAS LIVING in the custody of Ancona at the friary of Forano with Brother Conrad of Offida, his close friend and a most virtuous man. One night as he meditated on the Passion of our Lord, he was sorely smitten with compassion. In spirit he pondered on Christ on the Cross, his grieving Mother and blessed John the Evangelist alongside the Cross; and on the other side Saint Francis marked with the holy stigmata. In a spirit of devout curiosity he began to wonder which of these three had felt the most grief at Christ's Passion.

As he lingered in doubt weeping copiously, there appeared to him as he watched the most radiant Virgin

Mother of God, along with Saint John the Evangelist and holy Father Francis bearing the same stigmata as the Crucified one, both clad in magnificent garments; but the raiment of blessed Francis exceeded the garment of blessed John in beauty. At the sight of them Brother Peter, not without reason, was amazed, but blessed John reassured him saying: "Be comforted in the Lord, and fear nothing; for we have been sent by the Lord to console and to clear up your uncertainty. Know therefore, that however much more the blessed Virgin and I were grieved at the Passion of Christ which we beheld with mortal eyes, nevertheless after us blessed Francis grieved more than anybody. For that reason you realize that his sacred wounds raised him to greater glory above all others."

Then Brother Peter summoning up his courage asked why blessed Francis was wearing a more comely garment. The reply was: "Because while he lived he wore meaner clothing for Christ's sake." And with these words blessed John gave Brother Peter a very beautiful garment saying: "Accept this garment that your beloved Lord Jesus sends you." And when he clothed Brother Peter with the garment, he was filled with exceeding wonder, and not knowing what he was saying, shouted out: "Brother Conrad, Brother Conrad, come quickly and behold the miracles of God!" And at these words the vision faded. As Brother Conrad of Offida, his close and virtuous friend, hastened to his cell Brother Peter recounted to him all the details of the vision.

Chapter 75

How Brother Pacifico in prayer saw the soul of Brother Humilis flying up to heaven.

AFTER THE DEATH OF BLESSED FRANCIS there emerged Brothers Pacifico and Humilis, two blood-brothers of great perfection, and of outstanding and wonderful sanctity. When one of them departed this life at the friary of Soffiano, his brother praying in places afar off saw his soul rising straight up to heaven.

A few years passed by. The surviving brother was living at the said friary of Soffiano where his brother had passed away. Then at the request of the lords of Brunfort the friary was moved to another place. Translated also were the bones of the friars buried there. Then this brother with the utmost devotion taking up the bones of his brother, shedding copious tears, handling and kissing them with great reverence, washed them in wine and wrapped them carefully in a beautiful shroud.

The other friars observing this were scandalized at it, for although he was well-known for his great sanctity, he was merely honoring the bones of his brother with worldly affection. Mollifying them he said: "Do not think, beloved brethren, that I was prompted by mere worldly affection to show such great reverence to the bones of my brother, for on the day he died, as I was praying in a remote spot, I saw his soul ascending to paradise. These bones, destined some day to rest in paradise, I honor more than others."

Chapter 76

How Brother James of Massa saw all the friars minor of the whole world in a vision of a wonderful tree, and how he came to know the virtues, merits and sins of each brother.

IT WAS TO BROTHER JAMES OF MASSA that God opened the door of his secrets. Brother Giles of Assisi and Brother Marcus of Montino knew no worthier man. This too was the feeling of Brother Juniper.

I was under the direction of Brother John, and companion of the said Brother Giles. When I questioned him about certain matters for my own edification he said to me: "If you wish to be instructed in spiritual matters, hasten and have talks with Brother James of Massa." He also said that Brother Giles wished to be instructed by him; nothing could be added to his words or be withdrawn from them, for his mind had penetrated mysteries, and his words were the words of the Holy Spirit. "There is no man on earth whom I would so much like to see."

This Brother James, at some time in the ministry of Brother John of Parma, was once rapt and remained unconscious for three days, so that the friars began to wonder if he was dead. To him came the divine gift of knowledge and understanding of the Scriptures, the knowledge of things to come. To him I put the question: "If what I have heard about you is true, I beg you not to conceal anything from me. For I have heard that at the time when you lay for three days almost dead, God revealed to you among other things what was going to happen in the Order." For Brother

166

Matthew who was then minister of the province of the Marches, summoned him after that rapture and under obedience bade him tell what he had seen. Brother Matthew was a man of wondrous gentleness, holiness and simplicity. Frequently in conversation with the friars he told them: "I know a friar to whom God has revealed everything that will happen in our Order, and secrets, which if they were uttered could not be, I do not say understood, but scarcely believed."

The said Brother James revealed to me and told me among other things one very amazing thing; namely that after many things had been shown to him concerning the state of the church militant, he saw a very beautiful and extremely lofty tree. Its roots were of gold, its fruits were men, all of them friars minor. The number of principal branches corresponded to the number of provinces, and each branch had as many fruits as there were friars in that province. So he came to know the number of friars in the whole Order—and the separate provinces—their names, faces, age, duties, personality, rank, distinctions, their merits and faults. And he saw Brother John of Parma standing on the topmost branch in the middle of the tree. On the branches that grew around the central trunk stood the ministers of the various provinces. He then saw Christ seated on a mighty white throne, sending forth Saint Francis with two angels. And he gave Francis a chalice full of the spirit of life with these words: "Go, visit your friars and give them to drink of the spirit of life, for the spirit of Satan will arise and attack them; many of them will fall and be unable to rise again." Then Saint Francis came to administer the spirit of life as he had been bidden. Beginning with Brother John, the minister general, he gave him the full cup of the spirit of life. He accepted the full cup from the hand of Saint Francis and quickly and devoutly drank all of it. And when he had drunk he became as radiant as the sun. After him Francis offered to all, one by one, the cup of the spirit of life. Very few there were who received it with becoming reverence and drank all of it. Those few who reverently drank all of it assumed a sun-like radiance; those who poured some out all became black and dark, deformed, ghastly and horrible to look upon, resembling devils. Some drank part and poured out the rest; and according as each one received or poured away the spirit of life offered to them in the cup, so in corresponding measure they took on darkness or radiance.

But brightly outshining all who were on the tree was Brother John who, totally absorbed in contemplating the infinity of God's grace, perceived with the instinct of true enlightenment that a whirlwind and mighty tempest were making towards the tree. Descending from the top of the branch where he had been standing, he concealed himself in a more solid part of the tree trunk.

While there he watched and devoted himself to contemplation, Brother Bonaventure had climbed up to the place from which he had descended. He had drunk part of the chalice offered to him and poured away part of it. His finger-nails were turned to iron, sharp and cutting as razors. Leaving the place he occupied he wanted to rush and attack Brother John. When Brother John saw him he called on the Lord Jesus Christ. On hearing Brother John's call the Lord called Saint Francis and gave him a sharp stone and said: "Go and cut off the finger-nails of Brother Bonaventure with which he wants to rend Brother John, so that he cannot hurt him." So Saint Francis came and cut off the iron finger-nails of Brother Bonaventure. Brother John remained in his position radiant as the sun.

Then the violent whirlwind arose and struck the tree and the friars began to fall off. The first to fall were those who had poured out the whole content of the chalice of the spirit of life. Brother John and those who had drunk all the contents of the chalice were by divine power translated to a region of life, light and splendor.

Those who fell, already cast into gloom by the ministers of darkness, were taken away to abodes of wretchedness and obscurity.

He who had seen the vision understood the details of everything he saw. He saw clearly and reliably remembered the places, persons, ages and functions of each group, those blessed with light and those plunged into darkness. The whirlwind lasted, as did the fierce storm, permitted by God's justice, until the tree was torn up by the roots and crashed to the ground.

As the whirlwind and raging storm subsided there sprouted from the golden root of the tree shoots, all of gold, that produced golden flowers and fruit. As for the growth of this tree, its height, fragrance, beauty and virtue, it is better to preserve silence than to speak.

Here is one thing that sounded very remarkable to my ears as recounted by him who witnessed this vision. Do not fail to notice it; for he said that the manner of improving the Order would be entirely different. For the working of the Holy Spirit will choose uneducated young men, and unsophisticated ordinary persons who are looked down upon. Without precedent, without a teacher, in fact contrary to the training and personal character of those who teach, the Spirit of Christ will choose them and will fill them with a holy reverence and a very pure love of Christ. And when the Spirit has increased the number of such persons in various places, then it will send forth a wholly pure and saintly shepherd and leader, conforming to Christ. To the praise and glory, etc.